Expression ~ Surrender ~ Patience ~ Transformation ~ Celebration

Book Design ~ Your Divine Pathway
www.yourdivinepathway.com

Edited By ~ Christine Burk

Photography By ~ Experts Advantage
and Brenda V. Nixon

Published By ~ Your Divine Pathway

Made in the USA
2014

ISBN:069231928X

Altars Of Intentions

What You Desire Can Be Fulfilled

A Devotional Book For Women

Create A Personal Sacred Altar for Your Focus and Intentions

By

Brenda V. Nixon

Friendship ~ Cherish ~ Trust ~ Dance ~ Laugh ~ Love ~ Gratitude

Divine Dedication

I dedicate this book to you and all of my Goddess Sisters

It is my deepest desire that this book will inspire you to be creative

It is my deepest desire that your dreams become your reality

It is my deepest desire that you are happy

It is my deepest desire that you live with

Joy ~ Grace ~ Ease

Transformation ~ Appearance ~ Character ~ Function

My Divine Intentions

My intention for this book is to share my love for creating sacred altars, and to share my experience of grace that I have received from constructing and enjoying them. I wish to inspire you by making sacred altars an easy, fun, and a natural way to express yourself.

When done with heart, the creation of a sacred altar can aid in re-claiming your birthright, which is love and freedom.
Your birthright is the right to have your dreams come true.

By using the ten easy steps of altar creation, along with your divine *intentions* and *focus,* you can live your dreams, gain personal empowerment and be connected to your heart. This book contains some *gems* from the brilliant teachers who have inspired me to live with more joy, grace and ease.

How To Use This Book

Have an intention that "touches your heart."

Use my examples as a starting place ~ then and add your own ideas too.

Develop awareness in your daily life by staying in the *present moment.*

Be aware of your thoughts as being either positive or negative.

Use your altar daily for your focus and manifest your dreams.

Create Devotional Blissiplines that keep you anchored to your intentions.

Believe in your desired outcome. Do not allow yourself to think of failure.

Mentally visualize in vivid detail, your intention as an established fact.

Merge with it completely.

Surrender ~ Power ~ Universe ~ So ~ Be ~It

Divine Contents

CHAPTER ONE
Your Soul Answers You

On my first trip to Northern India in 2005, I experienced a tremendous Heart opening, while I was viewing a sacred altar at the Lakahmana Temple located in Khajuraho city.

Walking up the grand staircase to the altar, I could *feel* the energy imbued within this ancient structure. As I entered the temple, which dates as far back as 930-950 A.D., I noticed the huge, hand-carved stone pillars that were on either side of the doorway. The fine detail that went into these carvings was astonishing. I could see each elaborate stroke, and each one seemed to sing a song of timeless wisdom to me. I felt so much appreciation and gratitude.

As I gently touched the cold sandstone wall with my fingers, I was overwhelmed with deep feelings of admiration and awe. As I felt the smooth surfaces, I could almost hear the ancient sounds of the sandstone being chipped, carved and smoothed. Trying to describe such astounding works of art is simply impossible. These things must be seen and experienced directly. It was an atmosphere that was breathtaking.

The entire temple was something even grander to behold. The brilliance of the space was magnificent. The place felt alive and vibrant. In the design, no detail was left out. Each square inch was stamped with its own blueprint of uniqueness and spirit for future generations to witness and honor.

Once the official temple tour had finished, I was able to spend time just "being" in the space and connecting to the shrine. It was a time to sit, meditate and take-in the encounter of this majestic Temple.

I noticed that there were three statues, side-by-side. Bhagvan, who possesses fortune, is a divine and holy God. Lakshmi, the Goddess of fortune, was positioned in the middle next to Bhagvan. On the other side of Lakshmi sat Bhagvan Vishnu, the Master of ALL beyond past and present, and is the destroyer of all existences.

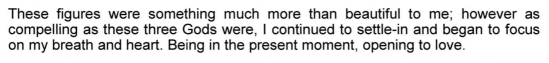

These figures were something much more than beautiful to me; however as compelling as these three Gods were, I continued to settle-in and began to focus on my breath and heart. Being in the present moment, opening to love.

I sat quietly, consciously practicing opening my heart to the Divine. With each inhale and exhale, I kept my intention on my *heart* as I sat in front of this sacred altar. I became very still and as I did, I had a sensation which I can best describe as follows. Imagine a veil over my head that blocks me from clearly seeing, and imagine it beginning to slowly lift. This sensation continued until I could not only *see* this brilliant altar and shrine before me, but I could also *feel* it, deeply. It was *alive* and I was *alive* with it. The lifting of this 'veil' that was now completely gone, had left me with the ability to see and feel like never before.

In the next instant, my entire body felt flush. I could feel intense emotion bubbling-up inside of me. I felt a pulsing rush come over me. I can describe it best by saying, what I called it at the time, "Overpowering Love." It came on so suddenly that, right then, I had no idea what was happening. It was beyond any known experience I have ever had.

My heart was bursting wide open. It was actually happening. It was a real event for me. Just as crying is a tangible experience in its own way, so was this. There was no separation between my Heart and anyone else's Heart. I felt as though my *heartbeat* was one and the same with the *heartbeat* of the world and with the *heartbeat* of the universe. I was actually in that moment, being one with the Divine. It was my first experience of such a *direct experience* with… *everything*.

My husband was by me witnessing this powerful expansion. Somehow, he could comprehend the opening that I was experiencing in front of this ancient sacred altar. He understood and he acted in a very special way. He watched over me and held the space around me as reverent. For him, to witness me this way was a sacred event. He was deeply moved.

I was over come with emotion. In deep connection with all of life, I began weeping. Tears streamed down my cheeks. In that moment of union, I will never forget the *truth* of me. I experienced Union with my Eternal Self and awakened Divine consciousness.

I felt deeply touched to embrace it. I was in my knowingness of pure Divine Love. Without any doubt I knew and I still *know*, that I am *pure love, unconditional love*. Even using these words, I feel, that there are no words which could possibly portray what I experienced.

The transmissions which I received at the divine altar that day were many.
I still feel they are gifts, my treasures. I received serenity. I received the clarity of knowing and of feeling my own true heart. I received the freedom to be *ONE-ness*. I received what it feels like to surrender and to embrace surrender with my entire body. I received pure divine grace.

Upon returning home from my trip to India, I began my quest to create sacred altars for my heart felt intentions. Over the past few years, as miracles became my reality, I began to share with others the graciousness a sacred altar can gift.

A Sacred Altar of any kind can greatly affect anyone, who is open to receive the infinite messages meant for them.

Sacred Altar And Space

How would it feel to create a sacred space, an altar that enables you to create and anchor your communications, focus and your intentions? What if this sacred space could help you to hear your messages and form the life you desire?
What if it supported you to become *unstuck* and feeling *hopeless* in your life?
If it really helped you, wouldn't that be simple and exhilarating?

Your sacred space, your self-made altar, helps you to intensify your focus. Your altar draws your attention into creating in a natural and steady way. The outcome is greater clarity, empowerment and results in an easy, joyful creation.

What if it was that easy and enjoyable? What if, your intention for your relationship, career, health, wealth or whatever you dream of, could simply be envisioned, symbolically created and then manifested? Now more than ever, it is that easy! A sacred altar or space that is your own creation, is a way to ask the *Divine* for inspiration and grace. It is a way to infuse these qualities into your life.

A sacred altar is a place where you choose. It is a place where you express yourself freely through symbolic objects, meditation, dance, chanting, song, and prayer. It is your majestic temple, it is your place to hold reverent.

Your sacred space is the foundation for your creations, and it is also a place to just 'be.' When the thrust of creation comes together with the stillness of being, intentions become reality.

Right now, your soul is using your body as a vehicle of expression for your life's journey. Your altar will be the vehicle that carries the expression and fulfillment of your heart's desires both personally and professionally. When you connect deeply with your true essence, you can manifest anything.

You create your life, and you are responsible for creating your connection to the Divine. You will awaken to gratitude, joy, love and freedom.

Your altar is a daily reminder and facilitator. It keeps you consciously tethered to the powerful vortex that manifests your desired outcomes.

Personal Expression

In the Western world, it has become more popular for people to create sacred altars and spaces in their homes.

For thousands of years, churches and temples have performed services and rituals to establish their religions. Why? They know how powerful it can be to utilize an altar for the creation of a belief and for the fulfillment of expectations.

No matter what your religious beliefs are, your personal altar reflects your personal spirituality. You do not need to give up your belief in God, Goddess or any other Worship, nor do you need to take on the beliefs of others. Creation of a sacred altar or space is an intimate personal project and expression.

Intention ~ Focus ~ Heart

The first step is to decide what *type* of altar will serve you best. To do this, it helps to understand the three most influential factors that affect the creation of your sacred altar.

1. Your Intention. What is your desired purpose, dream or goal? Your intention is the guiding structure and it is the roadmap, for the results that you are seeking.

2. Your Focus. How is your ability to concentrate and observe closely, continuously and intently on the point of interest, which is whatever you aim to manifest? Your focus is the driving force behind your manifestation. What you focus on expands.

3. Your Heart. The most important thing to have when creating an altar is a desire from your Heart. What moves you? What touches you? What are you deeply longing for?

Natures Symbols

You can also use nature as a way to connect to the Divine.
Every element in nature is a manifestation of the Infinite and is in relationship with your Higher Self.

Every element in nature – your body, cells, gasses, liquids, minerals, plants, animals, the sun, the stars, our universe and the galaxy – is *always* working to cooperate with each other.

Every aspect of existence is interconnected. Everything is included.
Information is continually transported to your awareness through the most clean, efficient and direct channels of energy, and communication.   The questions are: do you 'hear' and understand the messages?   How can you better connect your conscious awareness to this pristine stream of Divine information?

Butterfly And You

The butterfly's life cycle is one of the mysteries in Nature that can hold understanding for your life. The butterfly's life stages mirror your own life phases. You can apply the lessons she has to offer to your own life.
Both you and the butterfly experience: intense growth, ravenous hunger, vulnerable transformation and miraculous expansion.

Both you and the butterfly experience transformation, which can be life changing that you are unrecognizable by its end.
The butterfly surrenders to the changes in her environment and within her body.
Can you accept the changes in your life as naturally as the butterfly does?

If you want to surrender to 'what is' as effortlessly as the butterfly, then the butterfly can become a useful symbol for you.   You can become inspired by her inspiration.

You can open to her quiet demonstration of: patience, soul, grace, growth, elegance, expansion, lightness, surrender, transition, resurrection, vulnerability, expression and celebration.

Emotionally ~ Mentally ~ Physically ~ Spiritually

Awareness Of Your Environment And Body

In every moment, you are either opening your heart, or you are closing your heart. For instance, as you are reading this, you are either consciously having awareness of your sensations and thoughts or you are closed and unaware.

The more you feel open to something – an idea, another person, a feeling – the more you will feel connected to it. When you are unconsciously not open to something, the more feelings of separation exist. It is painful when you feel a disconnect from people, places, things and beliefs in your life. A way to feel more connected to others is simply to open your heart. Opening your heart is an *intention* and an *action*. With your intention, you can soften your heart and let go of your judgments of how you think things should look or what they should feel like.

Your own intuition can guide you because underneath it all, you are Divine love. It is simple to open your heart. You know how to do it, even if you have temporarily forgotten.

You have a choice, and if you are willing to practice, you can create change in your life. Practice means: to make a habit, or do something repeatedly, to improve or maintain proficiency. You can practice opening your heart. You can practice feeling "oneness" in the midst of experiences when you do not necessarily want to feel connected. Yes, this can sometimes be easier said than done, but it is worth the BLISS that surely occurs when you open your heart.

Instead of thinking of the *discipline* of opening your Heart as "practice," you can instead think of it as your "Bliss-i-pline." A Blissipline is a practice or discipline, which ultimately results in BLISS – supreme happiness and peace.

Within this book, you will encounter "Devotional Blissiplines" suggestions at the end of chapter one and seven. Take some time to do them, and experience devotional moments for yourself.

Blessings

There are many blessings a sacred altar can gift you. In so many divine and surprising ways, your sacred space can serve to bless you. These blessings often may come in spectacular ways, such as my own experience at the Temple in India, yet often these blessings come subtly. I have noticed when I have joy and humility, I receive more blessings.

An altar helps you to be more aware of your environment, your desires and your intentions. You begin to notice more and to attune throughout our day to all of the sacred altars that exist in life. You begin to notice how you are continuously impacted spiritually, mentally, emotionally and physically. These are the messages.

Take a careful look around where you are right now.
What do you see?

Are your surroundings manmade or are you in nature?
Does it speak to you?
Can you hear it?
Can you taste it?
Can you smell it?
Can you feel the energy between you and what you are seeing?
How does your environment in your personal home serve you?
Are you going to places and doing things that *fill you up* or deplete you?
What do you focus your precious time and energy on?
What makes your heart sing?

Take a moment to really feel into these questions. Are you feeling inspired or burdened? How can you create more in your life of what you would like to experience?

As you become more consciously aware of yourself and your surroundings, you learn to feel the presence of life energy in your body. You will feel your *internal connection* to your life energy, and it becomes a natural state of openness and awareness for you. It is where you will discover your indestructible sense of *belonging*. This is truly a blessing.

You can be curious, not judgmental. You can allow yourself to simply feel what you feel. Where are you *comfortable* and *present* in your body and where are you not*?* This alertness deepens your *internal* awareness and helps support you in being more open to the *external* world.

You already have ways to increase your energetic awareness, such as walking on the beach, hiking in the woods, basking in the sun as it warms your body, or gently floating in a lake. Any activity, such as meditation that relaxes you also serves to increase your awareness and to open your heart.

Let's reclaim your *inner wisdom* by recognizing and honoring your gut feelings and your hearts desires. This too will open your heart. You will feel lighter and have more vitality, peace and joy.

The butterfly beckons you to keep your faith as you under go transitions in your life. Enjoy creating and using your sacred altar for growth, expression and celebration. You will emerge as brilliantly as the butterfly.

Devotional Blissiplines ~ Find More In Chapter Six

~ 'Heart Opening' meditation to enliven your heart to love.
~ 'Body Awareness' meditation to awaken your connection with your higher -self.

Passions ~ Desires ~ Manifestation ~ Transformation

CHAPTER TWO
Ten Easy Steps

Creating a sacred altar that reflects your inner values and your vision for the future, is as simple as following ten easy steps. Each step is straightforward and has fun choices. Choose and gather: your intention symbol, evoke your desires, communication bowl, devotional blissiplines, table and space, beautiful fabric, flowers and plants, then create and ignite your altar.

Each altar is a representation of both how you are currently feeling and how you are imagining your life to be. A sacred altar is an expression of your creativity, so your altar is a kind of vision board that depicts your current dreams and desires. Each object on the altar holds private meaning for a value you hold dear or for an outcome you desire.

Your can change your altar often. You can choose different altar themes according to what is presently important to you. Since your altar expresses what touches your heart, the kind of altar you make is limited only by your own imagination. Some examples of the different kinds of altars that you may create include altars centered around: relationships, children, pets, health and well-being, spirituality, abundance, prosperity, life changes, career, recognition, loved ones, those who have passed, goals, accomplishments, and so much more.

Your sacred altar is a way that you can express your intentions and create the balance that supports your universe.

~ Ten Easy Steps ~

1. Intention Symbol
2. Evoking Your Desires
3. Communication Bowl
4. Devotional Blissiplines
5. Table And Space

6. Beautiful Fabric
7. Symbolic Candles
8. Flowers And Plants
9. Create Your Altar
10. Igniting Your Altar

INTENTIONS ~ ELEMENTS ~ COMMUNICATIONS

Express And Harness The Creative Force For Your *INTENTIONS*

Intention Symbol ~
Qualities: *Any item that represents a feeling or a result you desire.*
Suggestions: Make a collage, collect shells or gather pictures. Use statues, figurines or deities that represent or evoke a particular quality or meaning. You may make something, buy something or find something – what matters is that the collected items have a heartfelt meaning for you.

Use Representations Of The *ELEMENTS* To Signify Your Meaning / Purpose

Air ~
Qualities: *Blessings, good wishes, changes, movement, hopes and dreams.*
Suggestions: Use anything that floats in the air or creates sound waves carried by the air. You may use a feather, a decorative fan, chimes, bells and incense.

Earth ~
Qualities: *Grounding, influences, supports and gives birth to new possibilities.*
Suggestions: Use rocks, stones, deities, metal, natural crystals, items made from wood or anything taken from the ground.

Fire ~
Qualities: *Brings passion for your manifestation, change and transformation.*
Suggestions: Use candles, oil lamp, aromatherapy lamp or incense.

Water ~
Qualities: *Represents your emotions, desires, spiritual, and material growth.*
Suggestions: Float flower petals in a glass bowl or use a small fountain or fishbowl. Display a transparent vase with flowers, so that the water can be seen.

Use Creative *TOOLS* And *PRACTICES* To Construct Your Hopes And Dreams

Communication Bowl ~
Purpose: *Holds the communications of your intentions*.
Suggestions: Use a small brass bowl, clay bowl, simple tray or crystal dish.

Evoking Your Desires ~
Purpose: *To bring forth your emotional feelings.*
Suggestions: Write a word or simple phrase using small un-lined pieces of paper, and place them in the bowl. Write something that evokes the feelings you would like to experience.

Devotional Blissiplines ~
Purpose: *Acknowledge and harness the aim of your altar*.
Suggestions: Dance, meditate, read or pray. You may do yoga or original movement. Be creative and use some of your own practices.

Vulnerability ~ Expansion ~ Elegance ~ Oneness

*Example of a handmade Spiritual Intention Symbol
using rocks, shells, words, feathers and a clay piece.*

CHAPTER THREE
Intention Symbol

Step 1~ Choose Your Intention Symbol

This is the most important step when creating your sacred altar. Choosing a symbolic item, which represents a personal desire and anchors the intention to an actual outcome.

It is best to choose a personal Intention Symbol that represents the *result* you most desire. Be creative and put your full heart into this step.

An intention is a goal, plan or idea. It is a wish with a focused outcome. An intention is created in your thoughts, and it is a vision of an outcome that you desire and see happening at some point in the future.
Your intentions are your dreams, held close to your heart.

Example of a framed 8x10 collage for a Relationship Intention Symbol

INTENTION SYMBOL IDEAS

Intending Abundance
~ Make a collage that inspires the feelings of abundance. Your collage can be made from pictures or words clipped from magazines.
~ Use your own pictures or beautiful artwork that you created.
~ Make a collage using real money taped to the cardboard backing of a 4x8 or 8x10 gold picture frame. Any domination of currency bills is okay.
~ Statue of Lakshmi, Goddess of Fortune and Abundance.

Intending Career And Success Fulfillment
~ Make or use an object that symbolizes and inspires the feeling of success for you.
~ Use a photograph or make a collage of words and/or pictures from a magazine that you cut out.
~ Create a certificate and fill-in what it is you are wish to receive. There are sites online where you can print them up or buy it from your local business store.
~ You may use a trophy, award ribbons, award pins or plaque.

Intending Life Changes
~ Find a picture that inspires feelings of support and ease in your transition.
~ Use a statue of Ganesh, remover of barriers or statue of Quan Yin, who hears and answers all prayers sent her way.
~ Make a collage, using pictures or words of how you want to feel for your desired outcome.
~ Choose a card from your Goddess Oracle Deck or another card deck that depicts the grace you desire.

Intending Close Relationships With Family
~ Make a collage with pictures and words clipped from magazines that evokes the feelings you want to create with another.
~ Create a collage with pictures of your family and put it an 8x10 picture frame.
~ Find an object that inspires the feelings you wish to experience.
~ Use an item that you got/bought or made together.

Intending Health And Well-Being
~ Make a collage that evokes the feelings of health, comfort, and happiness.
~ Create an art piece from nature using small rocks, wood or shells.
~ Find a picture of someone or something that inspires you to feel better.
~ Use a statue of Quan Yin.

Intending Increased Knowledge And Creativity
~ Find a picture of someone or something that inspires you.
~ Use a statue or picture of Saraswati that bestows creativity and knowledge or Ganesh offering wisdom and understanding.
~ Create a collage using pictures and words cut out from magazines.
~ Make an art piece using items that inspire the feelings you desire.

Intending Relationship / Marriage
~ Make a collage using pictures of you and your partner or a picture that represents or evokes the feelings you would like experience in your relationship.
~ Use the statue of Krishna, who exemplifies loving relationships.
~ Clip words from magazines or write your own and use them in your collage.
~ To enhance or attract a new relationship, add objects in pairs: two hearts, two stones, two flowers, two candles, etc.

Intending Spirituality
~ Make a collage of pictures and/ or words that evokes the feelings you want to receive.
~ Use a picture of a person that has the qualities you want to embrace such as - Christ, Buddha, Mother Mary etc.
~ A statue of Buddha, whom teaches the detachment from suffering.
~ Choose a healing crystal, gemstone or rock that carries the end result you wish.

A Personal Note About Statues

I use a variety of statues and deities, which I have collected from around the world on my altars. The most important thing to remember when choosing a deity is that it represents the *qualities* you desire.

For example, when I use the deity Lakshmi, Goddess of fortune on my Abundance Altar, my intention is to bring forth her grace and beauty into my life.

Another example, when I use the deity Quan Yin, on my Health And Well-Being Altar my intention is to evoke her compassion, also her love, grace, and trusting she hears and answers every prayer sent her way.

In traditional belief, a deity is a supernatural being, who may be thought of as holy, divine, or sacred. Some religions have one supreme deity, while other religions have multiple deities of various ranks and importance. When I create a sacred altar, I use a deity to awaken a feeling, quality or to bring a blessing.

Deities are often thought to be immortal and are commonly assumed to have distinct personalities, qualities and traits. They each have notable consciousness, intellect, desires and emotions comparable, but usually superior to those of humans. In this book, I share just a few of the many deities that you can choose from. Trust your intuition when selecting them for your intentions.

Qualities To Behold

You may choose to have a deity on your altar that represents a quality or a desire you wish to obtain. I find it enjoyable and meaningful to include representations of deities from many belief systems on my sacred altars.

Beauty ~ Good Fortune
Wisdom ~ Understanding ~ Acceptance
Love ~ Patience ~ Inner Peace ~ Compassion
Prosperity ~ Music ~ Fertility ~ Healing ~ Sexual Desire
Communication ~ Spiritual Understanding ~ Feminine Energy
Detachment From Suffering ~ Obstacles Removed ~ Soul-mate ~ Joy

SACRED GODS ~ GODDESSES ~ ANGELS

Apollo
Greek God, Prophecy, Light, Music and Healing

Archangel Gabriel
Helps with Creativity, Fertility and Communication

Archangel Michael
Rids Toxins associated with Fear

Archangel Raphael
Assists in Healing of the Body, Mind and Spirit

Archangel Uriel
Influence for making informed decisions and assists in Spiritual understanding

Athena
Goddess of Wisdom, Justice, Arts and Skill

Buddha
Teaches detachment from suffering through "Inner Peace and The Middle Way"

Christ
Teaches Love and Acceptance

Eros
Love, Sexual Desire, and Worshiped as a Fertility God

Ganesh
Removes Obstacles, Offering Wisdom, Prosperity, Prudence and Understanding

Hathor
Love, Beauty Music, Dance, Joy and helps bring Soul-Mates together

Isis
The Moon Goddess, Embodies Femininity,
Motherhood, Healing, Magic, Power

Kali
Brings Dissolution and Destruction - Destroys Ignorance

Krishna
Brings Blessings to all Relationships, especially Romantic Ones,
Assists in Spiritual Awakening

Kuan Yin- also known as Quan Yin
Brings Mercy, Compassion, Protection, Love, Grace and the Divine Feminine
Energy - also Hears and Answers Every Prayer sent her way

Lakshmi
Offers Wealth, Beauty and Good fortune

Mother Mary
Gives Love, Patience, Support, Help and Healing

Parvati
The mother of Ganesh offers Goodness, Power and Strength

Saraswati
Bestows Creativity and Knowledge

Shiva
Destroys and Regenerates

St. Gaetanus
Assists in Job Seekers and Unemployed People

Tara
Aids Smooth Travel and Safe Spiritual Journey

The Power Of Crystals And Gems

Crystals are powerful "beings" in their own right, so it is best to approach and handle them with awareness and respect.

Crystals efficiently absorb and transmit energy – beyond what we can see or measure.

A primary function of any crystal is to cleanse and transmute negative energies. You may use your sacred healing crystals, gemstones, and semiprecious stones along with your personal Intention Symbol to magnify the fulfillment of your desires.

Crystals and semiprecious gemstones besides being decorative all carry healing properties when used for your intended purpose. The more you understand about them the more effective they are.

Crystals are constructed from seven possible geometric forms: triangles, squares, rectangles, hexagons, rhomboids, parallelograms and trapeziums.

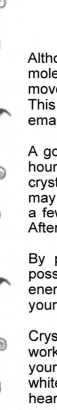

Although a crystal may look outwardly solid and still, it is actually a moving molecular mass, vibrating at a certain frequency. The unique structure and movement of each crystal is what gives that crystal its energy, and its frequency. This frequency is the pulse, which draws and absorbs as well as emits and emanates.

A good way to begin cleansing your crystals is by covering them in salt for 24 hours. This helps to wipe the crystals of previous activity. It will not wipe the crystal of its primary function, as this is embedded in the crystal's structure. You may also cleanse your crystals by placing them in the sunlight or full moonlight for a few hours. Perhaps have a "crystal day," devoted to preparing your crystals. After cleansing your crystals, meditate on attuning your crystals to your intentions.

By passing your own frequency through your intentions and emotions, it is possible to program a crystal. In fact, crystals are always receiving and giving off energy, whether or not you intentionally participate in the process. By engaging your own awareness it is possible to dedicate and program your crystals.

Crystals are highly responsive. You will experience this for yourself the more you work with them. The easiest way to attune your crystal is to hold it in the palm of your hand. Take a breath in and exhale. Gently close your eyes and visualize white light surrounding it. Let the energy flow through your hand and into your heart. Say, "May this crystal be used by me with light and love for the highest good for all." As the energy begins to expand, allow yourself be open to the *Divine higher guidance*. Be specific about what you desire. Take another breath in and exhale, when you are ready open your eyes. Your crystal is now attuned to your energy.

In this book I have just scratched the surface about the crystal kingdom. There is a lot of information available if you are interested to learn more about it, and I recommend that you do. The gifts these precious gems offer are powerful and it will add to your intentions and healing.

Treasured Gifts

My own crystals and semiprecious stones have become potent, personal treasures. A decade ago, I traveled with my family by a small boat along the Stikine River in Wrangle Alaska to a remote Garnet mine, where I gathered my stones. The whole family helped chip and chisel out the precious stones being careful not to damage them. It was an amazing experience for all of us.

I use them on my altars for devotion and love. I also wear ring that a dear friend had specially made for me using a garnet that I chipped from the huge rock walls.

A few years later during a visit to Montana, I dug for my Quartz Crystals that I use on my altars for planetary healing, creativity and peace. Shoveling dirt and digging to uncover buried crystals was wonderful, thrilling, profound, and adds to my special feelings of the stones. I have gifted my family and friends with these precious gems. It is powerful and meaningful to find and use your own gems and crystals in this devotional way.

Precious ~ Beauty ~ Creativity ~ Clarity ~ Peace

Crystal Connection Meditation

Items needed; candle, crystal(s), area near your altar, and a comfy seat.

Light your candle. Sit in a comfortable position, holding your crystal(s) in both of your hands. Keeping your eyes open, gently breathe and with each inhalation you take in, let peace flow through your body. As you gently breathe out, release any stress or tension you may be feeling. Let go, breathe and relax.
With each breath, allow peace and love to become your mantra. Gently gaze at your crystal(s). Notice its color, shape, size, and texture. Be open.

Close your eyes and feel its vibrations passing into your hands and into your heart. With your intention and imagination, enter into the inner beauty of the crystal, and allow yourself to explore and contemplate the energies you find there.

Set your intention and allow the crystal(s) to support you. Let the crystal teach you. Be with it, explore and enjoy! When you feel complete, gently open your eyes. Your crystal(s) are now ready for you to place them upon your sacred altar.

HEALING CRYSTALS AND GEMS

Agate
Encourages Awareness, Promotes Increased Energy Levels
Use it to 'Ground Yourself' when needing stability

Amethyst
Good for Meditation, Rituals and Self-knowledge
Promotes a good nights sleep

Aquamarine
Aids Self-Awareness and Self-Responsibility
Helps to break self-defeating habits

Bloodstone
Revitalizes Dying Hopes and Stimulates Dreaming
Helps to Ground Heart Energy

Citrine
Energizes Every Level of Life
Absorbs, Transmutes and Dissipates Negative Energy
Promotes Confidence and Balance

Diamond
Amplifies Wisdom, Purity and Perfection
Promotes Honesty, Loyalty, and Abundance

Emerald
Balances Partnerships
Enhances Psychic Abilities

Garnet Crystals
Regenerates the Body and Simulates Metabolism
Inspires Love, Devotion, Self-Confidence

Jade
Promotes Feelings of Unconditional Love, Attracting Loyalty and Support
Bolsters the Immune System (*keep a piece by your bed!*)

Moonstone
Promotes Emotional Balance, Passion
Sexual Energy, Emanates Lunar Qualities

Quartz Crystals
The "Master Crystal" that relieves Pain and Increases Planetary Healing
Stimulates Creativity, Clarity, Peace and Harmony

Rose Quartz
Promotes Unconditional Love and Infinite Peace
The most important crystal for the heart, because it aids your Heart Chakra

Sapphire
Focuses and Calms the Mind
Releases Unwanted Thoughts and Mental Tension

Topaz
Promotes Truth and Forgiveness
Abundance and Good Health

Tourmaline
Clears, Balances all Chakras
An effective healing 'wand' that focuses healing energies in a particular direction

Turquoise
Offers Strength After Illness
Promotes Success and Fulfillment

White Coral
Guards against Accidents, Acts of Violence, Theft, Possession and Sterility
Enhances Resilience and Bravery

Evoking Your Desires

You may write the words "Health, Abundance or True love."

A Few Simple Phrases Could Be

"I am supported and grateful for the grace and ease that is flowing through me."
"I know the world is abundant and I am and I feel worthy of experiencing it."
"I love and believe in myself and I love and believe in others."
"I am connected with my body, mind, and spirituality."

CHAPTER FOUR
Evoking Your Desires

Step 2 ~ Write Your Desires

To evoke what you desire, write one word, several words or a simple phrase that has an emotional response for the *end result* that you desire.

You have to call forth your desires, from the Universe. You must tell it what you want, not just think about it. Evoke your dream as a fact.

It is important to understand that everyone has both *passive* intentions and *active* intentions. A passive intention is something you wish, but do nothing to bring about. An active intention is a desire that you put your thoughts, feelings and actions behind.

A passive intention lacks focus and action. Passive intentions are expressed through weak and passive thoughts, such as, "I wonder what it would feel like… maybe… someday… I'm not sure which one is best… etc."

Active intentions are a clear visualization of an outcome, strong detailed thoughts, thinking, and follow through actions. "I can do this… this is what I want… I see myself doing (<u>fill in the blank</u>)."

Your intentions are your link to your goals. Taking time everyday to renew your intentions and to practice some of your Devotional Blissiplines will ensure that your life will change in all of the ways that you desire.

According to your own beliefs, you may want to use Tarot, Medicine, Goddess or Angel cards on your altar. Change the cards as often as you like.

You may also use small objects such as gems, coins or jewels, which symbolically represent the feeling you desire and place them in your Communication Bowl.

Knowledge And Creativity Communication Bowl

When you use your Communication Bowl, you are conveying information through the exchange of thoughts, messages, writing and behavior.

Request To Receive From The Divine Example
"To feel and be inspired as I learn more ways of being
creative with everything I do."
"To inspire others in creating the life that they dream of having."

CHAPTER FIVE
Communication Bowl

Step 3 ~ Choose Your Communication Bowl

The Communication Bowl is a symbolic container that is meant to hold your desires for the Divine. This special bowl is the chalice that holds your dreams and defines your focus. Place your Communication Bowl in what you consider to be the center of your altar and your Intention Symbol(s) are placed behind it.

To use your Communication Bowl, write down a word or a phrase that will evoke the emotional response you would like to experience.

When choosing your Communication Bowl, keep in mind the size of your altar and the material that the container is made of. Use a small crystal dish, gemstone bowl, wooden bowl, brass tray, clay bowl, metal container, small decorated plate, pedestal or a pewter cup.

Devotional ~ Actions ~ Fulfillment ~ Bliss

By simply lighting a candle, giving a heart-felt bow and performing a simple practice of some kind, you take care of your inner life. You bring your sacred self present.

CHAPTER SIX
Devotional Blissiplines

Step 4 ~ Practice Devotional Blissiplines

Creating whatever it is you truly want in life is a simple equation.
Heartfelt intentions + committed actions = fulfilled dreams. A Devotional Blissipline is any intentional practice you choose to do that will get you closer to your goals and ideals. It requires your heartfelt intentions and engages you in committed actions. So the goal and result of a Devotional Blissipline is the *fulfillment* of your dreams.

You may already have some of your own sacred practices that have supported you and I invite you to use those along with the eight Blissiplines in this book.

Devotional Blissiplines are a way to keep your commitment to yourself and to use your altar on a regular basis. It is a personal spiritual practice that links your deep desires with your daily life. Spend ten to thirty minutes a day in devotion.

Starting a daily meditation, dance or spending time in nature is a great way to connect you to your altar, your dreams, and your daily life.
If possible, do your Blissiplines in front of or near your altar to infuse it with your energy and to keep you tethered to your sacred space.
You will come to realize that your sacred altar is, itself, a Devotional Blissipline.

Devotional Blissiplines Examples

To reach your full potential, to make your heart sing, it is best to create using clear intentions and Devotional Blissiplines to manifest whatever you desire.
There are *eight* suggested Devotional Blissiplines in this chapter to get you started. They are designed to be joyful and to support your daily devotions.

For instance, if your desire is to have financial *Abundance* in your life, then you could use the *"Intentions Meditation"* and you can add these words; "I love and believe in myself and I love and believe in others. I know the world is abundant and I am and I feel worthy to receive (*fill in the blank*)."
You may also write words or phases on small pieces of unlined paper and drop them into your Communication Bowl.

If your intention is to improve your *Career And Success*, then the *"Heartbeat Meditation"* will remind you to stay connected to what really stirs you, what inspires you and what makes your heart burst wide open with delight.

Perhaps *Life Changes* is what you are going through. Then a simple way to feel more supported while you are in transition is by using the *"Grounding YourSelf"* meditation, in front of your sacred altar.

If your desire is for *Health And Well-Being*, in that case, you may use the *"Body Awareness Meditation"* and/or the *"Star Exercise"* in front of your sacred altar or an open window. Be sure to enhance your Blissiplines by writing in your healing journal daily any feelings, wins, or realizations that you are experiencing.
Keep these writings on or near your altar.

Deep down maybe your desire is for a loving *Relationship or Marriage*. You may want to use the *"Sacred Dance"* Blissipline and dance all around your altar area to awaken your love to the Divine, and send love through your heart to others.

If your desire is for *Spiritual Growth,* use the *"Opening Your Heart"* Blissipline.
You may journal, and have a daily spiritual reading. Your books may rest upon your altar. Be curious and keep coming back to your heart again and again.

Devotion ~ Nature ~ Pure ~ Gracious

You may want to mix and match the Devotional Blissiplines in this book to arrive at what suits you best. Soon you will be enjoying, creating, and looking forward to your daily sacred altar devotional time.

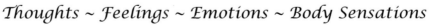

Thoughts ~ Feelings ~ Emotions ~ Body Sensations

For centering and accepting ' what is' in the moment, being and feeling happy with yourself and your environment. This may be used anytime and anywhere you find yourself feeling out of sorts and need support.

Acceptance

1. Stand in front of the area, where you are going to create your sacred altar or space. Stand with your legs shoulder width apart and your knees slightly bent. Stand in a manner that is both intentional and comfortable. Allow your arms to rest comfortably at your sides.

2. With your eyes open, take a deep breath in. As you inhale, imagine that you are taking in cleansing white light. As you exhale, allow all of tension and stress to leave your body.

3. Inhale another breath of cleansing white light. As you exhale, imagine that you are expanding outward as your breath releases. Take another inhale of cleansing white light, and exhale.

4. Notice any *thoughts* you may have. Whatever your *thoughts* are, choose to be okay with them. Say to yourself, "I accept that."

5. Notice any *feelings* you may have. Whatever your *feelings* are, choose to be okay with them. Say to yourself, "I accept that."

6. Notice any *body sensations* you may have. Whatever your *body sensations* are, choose to be okay with them. Say to yourself, "I accept that."

7. Inhale a deep final cleansing breath. Release your breath with an, "ahhhhh," sound. (*This is an ancient sound that may move negative energy from your body and replace it with feelings of freedom and joy.*)

When you are finished, allow yourself to relax and to feel the sense of your own creativity flowing through your veins. Feel your body vibrating with fresh energy. Notice any new awareness you may have and 'accept them.'

Calming ~ Conscious ~ Sensations ~ Understanding

Taking just a few minutes to "check in" with yourself to discover where your attention needs to go to relax. Begin to create an awareness with-in yourself daily.

48

Body Awareness Meditation

1. Sit in a chair with your eyes closed and with your bare feet on the ground.

2. Begin to go inward by focusing your awareness on the *inside* of your body.

3. Be open to discovering new awareness. Use your breath by following each inhalation with your attention. Follow your breath as it goes down into your lungs. Each time you inhale and exhale begin to go deeper inside.

4. Now allow your attention to widen. Check in with the rest of your body. What do you notice? Do you feel any sensations, pain or numbness? Allow your attention to start at your head and neck, what do they feel like? Is your neck tight? Does your head feel heavy? How do your eyes, cheeks, mouth, jaws, teeth, gums, tongue and throat all feel like? Are they relaxed, tight or uncomfortable?

5. Just notice. As you notice, begin to gently breathe into each and every area.

6. Move your attention to your heart area. How does your heart feel? Can you feel it beating? Does it seem to have a particular rhythm, color or feeling? Breathe into your heart. Breathe from your heart.

7. Move your attention to your chest, upper back, arms, hands and fingers. Notice any thoughts and feelings that appear. Begin to breathe into these areas of your body, taking your time.

8. Move your attention to your backbone, spine, pelvis, upper legs, thighs, knees, calves, feet and toes. What do they feel like? Do they feel connected and strong? Notice any thoughts and feelings that may appear. Begin to breathe into these areas of your body, taking your time.

9. Take one more scan of your whole body, starting at your head and working your way down. Simply notice, without judgment, any difference between your thoughts and feelings now compared to when you first sat down. Are you more relaxed, fidgety or serene?

10. Take a final deep cleansing breath. When you are ready, gently open your eyes. Thank yourself for taking some time to be with you!

Contact ~ Center ~ Universal ~ Life Energy ~ Harmony

The best time to perform this simple yet powerful exercise is in the morning, immediately after waking up and at night just before going to bed.
It is wonderful to perform this exercise in front of an open window.
The entire procedure should only take 3 – 5 minutes.

Star Exercise

1. Standing straight, yet relaxed, stretch your arms out to the side of your body. Bring your arms level with your shoulders, and spread your legs wide enough to match your arms.

2. Keep your head erect. Your body will be in the shape of a five-pointed star. Your whole body should remain engaged, yet not tense.

3. Turn the palm of your left hand up. Turn the palm of your right hand down. The upturned palm of your left hand receives Universal Life Energy, which is directed from Space towards the Earth.

4. This exercise works automatically. There is no need to think about the Force flowing through your body. You may say to yourself: "I am one with Universal Life Energy. It is flowing through me now. I feel it."

5. Experiment with taking deep rhythmic breaths. Fill your solar plexus with air. Notice any effects you receive from different breathing styles.

6. The Universal Life Energy contacted through the Star Exercise is pure Life Force. It will not only stimulate and invigorate you, but it will bring you peace, balance and harmony.

7. When you are complete, allow your arms to rest at your side. Take a deep breath in and release. You are ready for the next part of your day.

Centered ~ Connection ~ Aligned ~ Soul ~ Now Moment
Grounding reconnects your body energies with the energy of the Divine.

Grounding Yourself

1. Stand tall or sitting up straight in a chair, with both bare feet flat on the ground.
2. Close your eyes and become aware of your breath.
3. Slowly deepen your breath, breathing in through your nose and out through your mouth.
4. Imagine that you are a mighty tree. In your imagination, visualize details such as your size and texture.
5. From your waist down, imagine your strong trunk and your deep roots. From your waist up, imagine your flexible branches and your rustling leaves.
6. Imagine your roots growing deeper and deeper down into the Earth.
7. Picture the energy of Earth as infinite bits of brilliant diamond dust sparkling all around. Imagine the diamond dust being absorbed into your roots, and see this energy rising up through your roots and into your trunk.
8. As you visualize the brilliant diamond dust rising up your trunk, stretch your arms up and out above your head just like the branches of your mighty tree.
9. Visualize the brilliant diamond dust continuing to rise and energize every branch and leaf on your tree and then tilt your head back so that your face is warmed by the sun and smile.
10. Take some deep breaths while standing or sitting with your head tilted back, your arms outstretched and visualize more and more brilliant diamond dust energizing you.
11. Stay in this position until you feel the new energy pulsating throughout your body.
12. Slowly return your head to an upright position and bring your arms down with your hands coming together in prayer position over your heart.
13. Give thanks in whatever way you feel is appropriate.

Breath ~ Meditative ~ Energizes ~ Balances

Throughout the day, notice your breath and your heart and how they beat as one.

Heartbeat Meditation

1. Sit in a comfortable position. Gently allow your eyes to close. Begin to focus on your breathing, allowing it to be relaxed and effortless.

2. Keep your attention on your breath. Trust the feeling of the air coming into your body. Be a witness to the air entering and leaving your body. Don't try to change anything in anyway. Let go of control. Relax and be with your breath.

3. Allow the meditative process to do all of the work. Your only job is to notice your breath. As you do this, it will naturally help your system to relax. The spiritual life force that dwells in your breath is infinitely wise, so the more absorbed your mind becomes in the movement of your breath, the easier it will be for the "spirit of life" to take care of you.

4. Once the rhythms of your heart and breath come into synch, gently tuck your thumbs underneath your four fingers to form a fist. Begin to squeeze your thumbs with a steady even pressure. This will deepen and strengthen your breathing. Notice how this affects your heartbeat. Do not effort your breathing. Simply, begin to squeeze your thumbs.

5. Continue squeezing your thumbs for a minute or two, and then begin to squeeze a bit harder for a few more minutes. The harder you squeeze the stronger your heartbeat and breathing will become. You may work with any amount of pressure that feels right to you at the time. Get to know your heart and breath better. Take your time with this process. Being with your heartbeat.

6. When you are ready, slowly release the pressure on your thumbs. Note that your heartbeat and breathing will continue to feel nearly as strong as they did, while you were squeezing. Take a final cleansing breath in, and release fully.

7. Gradually open your eyes. Stay relaxed, so you may remain in this wonderful state as long as possible, connected with your breath and heart, as one.

Dream ~ Idea ~ Intention ~ Ambition ~ Purpose ~ Goal

Use this simple meditation often, especially when you have a burning desire.

Intentions Meditation

1. Sit in a comfortable position. Close your eyes, and quite your mind. When your mind is quiet, your subconscious is more open to receiving your intentions.

2. Observe your breath to help quite your mind. Gently breathe.

3. Envision in your mind, with as much detail as possible, exactly what your intention is.

4. Add as much description as possible to your vision. Include: sounds, smells, tastes, feelings, movements, etc.

5. Using clear and concise statements, narrate your vision. Say your intention aloud. Create a Mantra to use if you like.

6. Allow your entire being to become immersed in your intention. Feel it on all levels, as if it has already become your reality. Hold this feeling strongly for 15-30 seconds.

7. Keep breathing evenly, while staying connected to your intention.

8. When you are ready, open your eyes with a smile. So be it!

Unity ~ Closeness ~ Affinity ~ Oneness ~ Divine

You may do this Devotional Blissipline anytime, anywhere – even right now!

Opening Your Heart

1. Take a few relaxed breaths in and release.

2. Choose one thing in the environment you are currently in – you may pick a chair, picture, cup, pencil, tree, flower, anything. Choose something that you are not already in love with.

3. Begin gazing at the object with love. Choose to love it. Intend to love it as much as anything else in your life. Intend to love it as much as the person you love most in your life.

4. Keep looking at the object. Keep intending, as best as you can, to LOVE it. Open your heart and let that object in, loving it deeply. Keep intending to love.

5. If any other thoughts come into your mind, simply re-focus your thoughts, and continue to intend to love your object.

6. Continue to do this until you are able to love it like you have never loved before.

7. Be open to loving it. Being consciously open to loving something or someone is a way to experience "oneness."

8. Keep breathing. Relax into this moment of being open.

9. Continue this Devotional Blissipline until you feel that there is an instant, where you felt "oneness" or "love" with your object.

10. Whatever your outcome is, remain open and okay with it. Use this simple practice often, and it will help open you to more possibilities.

Movement ~ Express ~ Enhances ~ Experiences

This Sacred Dance Blissipline will guide you through opening your heart as you move your body. Your dance can express your love for yourself, another or for the Divine.

Sacred Dance

1. To begin, light the candles on your altar. In your own way, offer a simple gesture toward your altar to signify the beginning of your sacred movement time. The gesture may be a simple bow, a prayer – whatever you feel that will support your sacred dance.
2. As the music begins, take a few deep breaths. As you release each breath, allow yourself to smile. Relax and 'be' with the music.
3. Begin to move. Stay relaxed. Allow the music to take you for a dance. Allow any movement that naturally arises to be expressed. Just be easy with it. There is no certain way to move. There is no right way or wrong way to move. There are no special arm motions or special steps. The only thing you need to do is to move with the music.
4. As you allow the music to begin to sweep you away, think about the person, who you love most in your life. The person who comes to mind, may be alive or passed on. Put your *attention* on them as you dance and move your body.
5. Continue to move. As you do, open your heart and 'let them in.' Really let them in, as you move in this sacred dance. Dance in their love. Dance with your love for them.
6. Continue to consciously open your heart, while you move your body. You may find yourself moving differently now. Maybe you are being touched in such a way that your movement is slower, or faster. You may have some emotions arise. Let it all bubble up, and express it with your dance.
7. Keep opening your heart wider and wider. Stay with this for a while. Bask in the divine glory and light of moving and dancing, while feeling your love for another.
8. As you come to the end of your sacred dance, allow your movement to wind down, yet keep your heart open. Come to a resting position on the floor.
9. To end the session, you may sit or lie down. As you rest, imagine the Earth beneath you, tenderly supporting you.
10. Close your eyes. Put your attention on your breath. Consciously begin to breathe and with each inhale, breathe deeply into your belly. You can put your hands on your belly, so you can feel your breath. Simply surrender and breathe. When you are ready, inhale quietly, and exhale with an "ahhhhhh" sound. Do this three times.
11. You may wish to end your practice on your knees in front of your sacred altar. Give gratitude for all of the inspiration your dance and altar represents to you.

Sacred ~ Foundation ~ Treasures ~ Dreams ~ Reality

CHAPTER SEVEN
Table And Space

Step 5 ~ Create The Space That Holds Your Sacred Altar

When choosing the space where you will create your altar, whether it is in your home, office or outdoors, it is best to pick an area that has the most impact on you, as this will greatly enhance and affect the success of your altar.

Create your altar where it is aesthetically appealing to you, so that it improves the beauty of the room. Remember, by preparing the space, you are sending a message to the Universe that great *change* is going to take place!

The table you choose will need to be large enough to hold your items. The table will need to be in an area that is accessible and makes sense to you. These details are simple, yet important to consider. If your table is bothersome or awkward to navigate around, it will subtly distract from its purpose.

Perhaps be willing to use old items in new ways. You may have an end table you no longer use or a small table in your garage or attic that would be perfect. Look around your home or garden and find items that you would not have thought of to use: an old bench, a white stone pedestal, small antique table, small glass table, large serving tray, large brass platter, a chunk of beautiful wood that stands upright, etc. It is possible to transform almost anything from junk to treasure – be creative and have fun.

Behind your altar you can use decorative screens, beautiful fabric, a mirror, large picture, beautiful curtains, or wall hanging… the possibilities are endless.

Be sure to dust and clean the area with care. The more genuinely you clean, the more profoundly clear your space will be. Once you have cleaned and cleared the things and energies, which hold you to your past, you are ready to begin.

Magnetic energy runs from north to south and solar energy runs from east to west, creating a solar magnetic grid that covers the earth and affects every square inch of the planet. Many cultures use this directional energy grid for placement of important religious and iconic structures.

I recommend incorporating these directional energies in constructing your altar. Ancient cultures such as those of India, Egypt and Mexico have taken advantage of these energetic grids in the successful construction of their temples, shrines and altars for thousands of years.

You may use the eight directions, in the "Altar Directions Chart" along with a compass and your own intuition to locate the best possible location for your altar and all that goes upon it. If your home or space is not practical for the exact placement using the "Altar Directions Chart," then do your best to be close if possible. It is more important to follow your own inner guidance than to strictly adhere to any rules. All guidelines are suggestions that may aid in your creativity, but your sacred altar is your own private work of function and art.

The feelings and longings of your heart carry a vibration of their own. These feelings, when activated by your desire and directed by your intention, are what give your altar its aura. This can be a great benefit to the rest of your living space, which will move into a higher vibration, as it responds to the resonance of your sacred altar.

Notice how you feel, as you progress through this process of choosing where your altar will be created. Do you feel relaxed? Are you having fun? Do you feel nervous, unsure or uncomfortable? Are you questioning your choices? Do you find yourself asking, "Am I doing this *right*?"
Notice your thoughts, feelings, emotions and body sensations. Take a moment to be to be present during this process.

If any unpleasant emotions such as frustration, confusion or barriers arise along the way, take a deep breath in and release it with an "ahhh" sound. This simple action will surely help to move any negative energy, and replace it with a feeling of relaxation, joy and freedom.

Choosing the space and table for your altar is symbolic and is the supportive foundation for your dreams. Notice what you go through, and make the choice to keep it enjoyable. At any time, feel free to take a break and re-join the process at a later time and with a fresh perspective.

ALTAR DIRECTIONS CHART

North
Abundance

South
Career and Recognition

East
Health And Well-Being

West
Knowledge And Creativity

Southeast
Life Changes

Northwest
Relationships And Marriage

Northeast
Spirituality

Southwest
Universal Support

Devotional Blissipliness ~ Find More In Chapter Six

~ 'Acceptance Meditation' if you feel stuck preparing your altar.
~ 'Grounding Yourself' to support feelings of grounded connection.

Sacred Altars Are Designed To Express

Use a variety of fabrics, colors and textures to enhance your altars.
Let your choices reflect the variety and intensity of your intentions and dreams.

CHAPTER EIGHT
Beautiful Fabrics

Step 6 ~ Choose Beautiful Fabrics And Colors

Just as you choose an outfit at the beginning of each day or special event to best serve a purpose, the fabrics you choose for your altar will help craft and showcase the mood, feelings and intentions of your sacred space.

When dressing, you probably choose a practical outfit for the gym, a sharp outfit to impress for business and a comfy outfit for bed. The textiles you choose for your altar are just as functional, informative and expressive.

The feel, look and colors of your fabric will evoke specific feelings and reactions, so choose the cloth you will use according to emotions you wish to stimulate. These emotions are energies that are the fuel that bring your intentions to fruition.

Your fabrics may have a range of textures: smooth, soft, rough, bumpy, jeweled, woven, cool, quilted, slick, fuzzy, etc. What story does your fabric tell when you close your eyes and touch it?

When choosing your colors, keep in mind that colors are vibrations that affect moods, express feelings and stimulate emotions. Above all, you should like your colors. It is helpful to consider why you choose the colors you do for your altar. Are you choosing colors simply for aesthetic beauty, or do they have meaningful healing qualities and your altars intentions expressed through your choices as well?

By intentionally using colors, which match your type of altar and its healing intentions, you will deepen your awareness and bolster your outcome.

Look for fabric at yard sales, second hand stores, fabric stores, your house and your closet. I use beautiful scarfs, shawls, sari's, decorative pillow coverings, beautiful placemats, and table runners on my altars.

Before You Go Shopping

Look around your house before going out to buy something new. You probably already have a surprising number and variety of materials that you have collected over the years. Find the treasures you have stored on shelves and tucked away in drawers. These pieces all have a story of how they came your way, and will bring your sacred altar to life.

Meaningful To You, Pieces That Have Touched Your Heart

You may use decorative stands, trinket boxes, gemstone bowls, totem animals, crystals, precious gifts, keepsakes and heirlooms – the possibilities are endless.

The Fabric of Life is Truly Gracious
Alive with Texture
Soft and Bold
Bright and Shining
Depth and Daring
Exquisite and Playful
Detailed from End to End
The Thread That Connects Everything

FABRIC COLORS

Black
Seductive and Sophisticated
Absorbs Negative Energies

Blue
Instills Loyalty, Sincerity and Trustworthiness
Represents Kindness and Understanding

Brown
Strong, Sincere, Comfort, Grounding

Gold
Pathway to Inner Wisdom
Inspires the Power of Simplicity

Gray
Security, Reliability, Formal, Dignity

Green
Symbol for Peace, Tranquility and Calm
Gently Fosters Imagination

Indigo
Encourages the shedding of what is no longer required
Courage while facing fear and conquering weakness to break free

Orange
Promotes Clear Communication
Brings Forth Freedom of Expression

Pink
Promotes Healing, Compassion and Harmony
Color of Unconditional Love

Purple
Transmutation for Ceremony and Ritual
Evokes Creative Expression, Intuition and Spirituality

Red
Excites Emotions and Arouses the Senses
Energizes the Body and Motivates Action

Silver
Helps Achieve Balance and Harmony
Heals Hormonal Imbalances

Turquoise
Healing, Forgiveness, Independence

White
Symbolizes 'Enlightenment' and Carries the Wisdom of Ages
Represents all that is Positive

Yellow
Encourages 'Letting Go'
Promotes Friendship, Awakens Senses and Optimism

Colors Within

The Chakra system is a series of energetic portals along the central axis of your core being. Each energetic portal, or chakra, is an expression of energetic frequencies that are experienced through certain feelings, actions, attitudes, thoughts and emotions.

The Chakra Chart may be used as a guide to help you choose items for your sacred altar that represent and emanate the frequencies, mantras and colors you wish to include.

To illustrate, let's say you desire to make an altar for *Career and Knowledge*. The *Solar Plexus Chakra* is the center for *personal power, influence, and identity.*
Your *"mantra"* could be *"I am centered."*
You may want to add some *yellow* to your altar colors.

Perhaps your altar is for *Relationship or Marriage.*
The *Heart Chakra* is the center for *unconditional love, forgiveness, and healing.*
Your *"mantra"* could be *"I am accepted and I am loved."*
You may want to add some *green* and *pink* to your altar colors

Maybe your altar is for *Spirituality.*
The *Crown Chakra* is the center *for unity with the divine, wisdom and purpose.*
Your *"mantra"* could be *"I am growing and I am illumined.*
You may want to add some *violet* and *white* to your altar colors, to help your *thoughts* remain powerful.

Choose Essential Oils from the Chakra list that correspond with whichever Chakra you are using.

Note: There are more chakras than are represented here in this book, yet these are the most commonly known and a good place to start.

Crown Chakra ~ Violet
Brow Chakra ~ Indigo
Throat Chakra ~ Blue
Heart Chakra ~ Green
Solar Plexus Chakra ~ Yellow
Sacral Chakra ~ Orange
Base Chakra ~ Red

CHAKRA CHART

CROWN CHAKRA

Location	~ Top of Head
Color	~ Violet or White
Element	~ Thought
Essential Oils	~ Cedar, Frankincense, Lavender, Rosemary
Center For	~ Unity with the Divine, Wisdom, Purpose
Mantra, Violet	~ "I Am Growing"
Mantra, White	~ "I am Illumined"

BROW CHAKRA

Location	~ Third Eye
Color	~ Indigo
Element	~ Light
Essential Oils	~ Bay, Cedar, Cinnamon, Clay Sage, Jasmine
Center For	~ Inner Vision, Intuition, Manifestation
Mantra	~ "I Am Deep" or "I Am"

THROAT CHAKRA

Location	~ Neck
Color	~ Blue
Element	~ Ether
Sense	~ Sound
Essential Oils	~ Chamomile, Geranium, Myrrh, Peppermint
Center For	~ Communication, Integrity, Truth, Freedom
Mantra	~ "I Am Expansive"

HEART CHAKRA

Location	~ Center of Chest
Color	~ Green or Pink
Element	~ Air
Sense	~ Touch
Essential Oils	~ Jasmine, Lavender, Rose, Rosemary
Center For	~ Unconditional Love, Forgiveness, Healing
Mantra	~ "I Am Accepted" or "I Am Loved"

SOLAR PLEXUS CHAKRA

Location ~ Abdomen
Color ~ Yellow
Element ~ Fire
Sense ~ Sight
Essential Oils ~ Cedar, Chamomile, Ginger, Peppermint
Center For ~ Personal Power, Influence, Social Identity
Mantra ~ "I Am Centered"

SACRAL CHAKRA

Location ~ Navel / Pelvis
Color ~ Orange
Element ~ Water
Sense ~ Taste
Essential Oils ~ Cardamom, Geranium, Jasmine, Sweet Orange
Center For ~ Personal Creativity, Primal Feelings, Awe
Mantra ~ "I Am Satisfied"

BASE CHAKRA

Location ~ Base of Spine
Color ~ Red
Element ~ Earth
Sense ~ Smell
Essential Oils ~ Cedar, Frankincense, Myrrh, Sandalwood
Center For ~ Survival, Vitality, Grounding, Stillness
Mantra ~ "I Am Ignited"

Candle Containers

Candles also give off a tranquil feeling. This serene emanation can help evoke a renewed, positive influx of energy for your body, mind and spirit.

Choose a candle container shape that suits your altar. Use: pillar, taper, votive, candlesticks, tea lights, hanging candles, floating candles or candles in glass jars.

CHAPTER NINE
Symbolic Candles

Step 7 ~ Choose Your Candles

Candles are universally the symbolic and literal representation of light throughout all earth cultures and times. Candles have been lighting the way for all religions and for everyday use.

Their long meaningful usage makes candles the perfect representation of Light for your sacred altar.

The flame of a physical candle is a worldly version of the flame of the eternal. The use of candles on your sacred altar awakens an awareness of higher consciousness.

As already explained for your fabric in Step 6, candle color choice is important too because different colors represent and vibrate at varying frequencies. These vibrations converge with your own energies and assist you in manifesting your desires by balancing you and by protecting you from negative energies.
Of course, you may burn more than one candle and color at a time.
Light multiple candles in a clockwise direction or whatever direction you choose for the flow of light and energy.

CANDLE COLORS

Black
Disrupts Negative Energies and Thoughts
Deep Meditation, Peace and Silence

Brown
Removes Negative Omens and Patterns
Grounding

Blue
Forgiveness, Centeredness, Meditation
Resolution of Spiritual Issues

Dark Blue
Ability to Change Easily
Freedom to Act Freely

Gold
Unity, Good Fortune, Deep Understanding

Green
Financial Prosperity, Fertility
Balance, Confidence, Growth, Healing

Indigo
Enhances Spirituality and Intuition
Transformation

Lavender
Healing, Divine Freedom
Transmutation of Negative Energies and Karma's

Light Blue
Tranquility, Understanding
Health on All Levels

Orange
Encouragement, Vitality
Support for Careers and Friendships

Peach
Balance, Truth, Rejuvenation
Kindness

Pink
Honor, Love, Morality
Soul - Mate Attraction

Purple
Ambition, Progress, Power
Success in Business or in Organizations

Red
Health, Vigor, Sexual Love, Strength
Psychic Protection, Attaining Ambitions

Silver
Stability, Peace, Clear Thoughts
Persistence, Develop Psychic Abilities

Turquoise
Meditation, Self-Awareness, Calm
Ultimate Healing

White
Truth, Purity, Sincerity, Protection
Gives Peace and Comfort

Yellow
Enhances Communication, Clairvoyance and Learning
Improves Memory, Promotes Happiness

CANDLE CONFIGURATIONS

Triangle
Overcome Inner Conflict
Enhance Creativity and Good Fortune

Square
Grounds and Stabilizes
Enhances Compassion, Unconditional Love and Non-judgmental Behavior

Circle
Ultimate Protection
Symbolizes the Cycle of Life, Unity, Infinity, Birth and Rebirth

Cross
Align Energies, Links Heart Center
Balance Chakras

Diamond
Meditation, Harmony in Family and Home
Manifest Desires

Star ~ 5 Pointed
Strengthen and Heighten Spiritual Awareness
Help with Daily Life

Star ~ 6 Pointed
Protect, Balance, and Heals
Reconnects the Heart Chakra to the Mind

Star ~ 7 Pointed
Chakra Alignment, Healing, Self-Protection, Increased Energy
Harmony and Optimism

Triangle

Diamond

Square

Star 5 Pointed

Circle

Star 6 Pointed

Cross

Star 7 Pointed

Each configuration will give you varied effects and results.
Play with and make changes to attract and express what you desire.

Growing Your Own Flowers And Plants

Most of the flowers and some of the plants that I use on my altars come from my garden. I highly recommend if you are able to grow your own flowers to do so.

The energy and vibration from tending to them, and then using them for your sacred altar or space can have a positive and fulfilling effect for your experience. Choose plants and flowers that carry vibrations and healing for your intentions.

CHAPTER TEN
Flowers And Plants

Step 8 ~ Choose Flowers And Plants

Plants and flowers are life itself! Using fresh flowers will enhance vibrancy and strength to the fulfillment your intentions, so they are the perfect choice for your sacred altar. Live plants increase levels of positive energy. They promote happiness along with a relaxed and secure atmosphere. Flowers are also a beautiful symbol for sharing and caring.

There are a large variety of containers to use for flowers. Choose what works for you. Crystal, glass or see-through vases are especially effective because they allow the flow of color and light. You may add colored glass pebbles, small shells or decorative rocks to fill the bottom of your vase.

Using fresh fruit as an offering has been done for thousands of years in many cultures. On occasion, you may want to add fruit or sacred food, especially during anniversaries, celebrations, the full moon or Holidays.

When your flowers or plant dies, replace it with fresh ones to keep your altar 'alive with possibilities.'

83

FLOWERS ~ PLANTS ~ FRUIT OFFERINGS

African Violet
Banish Negativity

Aloe Plant
Physical Healing

Apple
Health, Vitality, Peace

Bamboo
Good Luck and Fortune

Bird of Paradise
Joy; Paradise Itself

Calla
Purity, Chastity

Carnation, Dark Red
Deep Love, Affection

Carnation, Light Red
Admiration

Carnation, Pink
Motherly Love

Carnation, White
Pure Love, Good Luck

Cherry Blossom
Spiritual Beauty

Corn
Abundance, Fertility, Blessings

Daffodil
New Beginnings, Un-equalled Love

Dahlia
Dignity, Forever Yours

Daisy
Purity, Loyal Love, Patience, Simplicity

Evening Primrose
Used as an Anti-Depressant

Fern
Ancient Symbol of the Wisdom of Mother Earth

Fuchsia
Humble, Love, Taste

Gerbera Daisy
Cheerfulness

Geranium
True Friendship

Hydrangea
Thank You for Understanding

Iris
Inspiration

Jade
Activates Financial Prosperity

Lilac, Purple
First Emotions of Love

Lilac, White
Youthful Innocence

Lily
Fertility; Long Lasting Relationships

Marigold
Exceptional Healing Powers

Oranges
A Prayer or Wish for Good Fortune

Orchid
Love and Beauty

Peaches
Immortality, Marriage, Tenderness

Peony
Honor, Nobility, Fertility, Peace

Pomegranates
Fertility, Unity Within Diversity

Rose, Orange
Enthusiasm, Fascination

Rose, Pink
Gentleness, Gratitude

Rose, Red
Love and Desire

Rose, White
Purification; Unconditional Love

Rose, Yellow
Friendship, Joy, New Start

Sunflower
Spiritual Attainment; Flexibility

Tulips
Adjustment, Aspiration and Resurrection

Dreams And Intentions

Your intention symbol, statues, crystals, fabric, candles, plants, flowers, and your communication bowl will reflect and amplify your focus of your Sacred Altar.

CHAPTER ELEVEN
Create Your Altar

Step 9 ~ Create Your Altar

There is nothing left to do, but to put it altogether and create your sacred space. You are prepared. Once you get started, you will find out how easy and powerful it is to give your dreams this stage.

Your altar will take on a life of its own as you begin to create it. Use everything you have gathered to give your dreams and intentions their new home.
There are eight altar examples in this book for you to reference, and soon you will be creating, and manifesting all your hopes and desires.

TIPS...

✱ It is best to create one altar for each intention at a time. That way, your focus will be like a *'bright spot light'* and your order to the Divine will not be diluted by confusion and overwhelm.

✱ Try not to have too many commands and demands, as it may impede the flow of opportunity.

✱ If you feel skeptical, doubtful, or critical while creating your altar, these feelings may block your manifestations. Be willing to offer these to the Divine, in your own way.

✱ Sometimes your lack of clarity or feelings of unworthiness will make what you are trying to create more difficult.

✱ Whatever you focus on grows, so it is your practice to keep your *attention* on your *intentions,* in a way that nurtures your connection to the Divine.

✱ Most of us have heard this truth before: your thoughts, words and beliefs impact the way you see your daily life in both *negative* and *positive* ways. Make the choice in each moment to be genuinely positive.

✱ It is important to keep your perceptions of *others* positive.

✱ Be willing to move past your *fears*, to your deepest heart longings and desires.

✱ Take time each day to acknowledge your altar, light your candles, dance, meditate, use your Devotional Blissiplines, your Altars Of Intentions cards and give a simple bow of gratitude as you walk past.

✱ Get started today and use the eight altar examples in this book as a place to begin, along with your own divine manifestation ideas.

Create

To bring something into existence ~ into being
To produce ~ generate ~ make ~ fabricate
To build ~ construct ~ originate ~ frame ~ shape

Abundance

Decide what abundance means to you, and how you wish to experience it with more money, a new home, having more clients or through inner wealth.

Tip... Do your best to be light hearted, being light hearted is angelic in many ways and it is easier than being stuck and unhappy.

ABUNDANCE ALTAR EXAMPLE

Intention Symbol ~ Use a beautiful gold frame; with a collage of dollar bills

Air ~ Small fan, bell or feather

Earth ~ Hindu statue or picture of the Goddess Lakshmi

Fire ~ Beautiful candles, green or gold containers

Water ~ Small fountain or a lucky bamboo plant

Fabric Colors ~ Green, gold, indigo

Aroma ~ Peppermint

Communication Bowl ~ Gold or brass bowl

Evoking Your Desire ~ Write a word or phrase for your intended result

Devotional Blissiplines
~ Intentions Meditation (*More bliss in chapter 6*)
~ Use your Altars Of Intentions Cards
~ Journal and write down five things that you are grateful for daily.

Placement Of Objects ~ Intention Symbol in the center of altar and your Communication Bowl in front of it. Candle and statue on the left side, flowers and other items on the right.

Additional Items ~ Dimond Gemstone

Career And Success

Do you want admiration, to be recognized by your peers, a high-paying career, or to feel fulfilled? Any limitations from your beliefs and thoughts can be diminished when you nurture your spirit with success.

CAREER AND SUCCESS ALTAR EXAMPLE

Intention Symbol ~ Use a picture or collage of the job, success or recognition you wish to receive.

Air ~ Standing chimes, singing bowl, incense

Earth ~ Use a small gold treasure box, jade plant

Fire ~ Yellow candle, tea lights in gold or red glass holders

Water ~ Orchids with a bit of yellow or white Daisies

Fabric Colors ~ Red, gold and white

Aroma ~ Frankincense

Communication Bowl ~ Copper or brass bowl

Evoking Your Desire ~ Write a word, phrase or use some other symbolic representation of what you are requesting to receive from the Divine and put it into your communication bowl.

Devotional Blissiplines ~ Heartbeat Meditation (*More bliss in chapter 6*)
~ Write down your innermost desires and needs to differentiate between vague yearnings of the ego, and what your true feelings really are. These are goals.
~ Use your Altars Of Intentions Cards.

Placement Of Objects ~ Intention Symbol in the center of altar and your Communication Bowl in front of it. Candle, chimes on the left side, flowers and statues on the right.

Additional Items ~ Ganesh Statue, Quartz Crystal, Aquamarine

Family

To inspire and bring your family closer together, create a Family Altar that can facilitate positive change. Having a new activity that has something in it for everyone can be fun, uplifting, and create deeper bonds.

FAMILY ALTAR EXAMPLE

Intention Symbol
~ Use a framed picture or create a collage of your family together or use another symbol that inspires togetherness.

Air
~ Incense holder or standing wind chime

Earth
~ Ganesh statue, Goddess or Tarot card

Fire
~ Yellow or blue candle holder

Water
~ Clear vase with fresh white roses, or white daisies or a small fish bowl.

Fabric Colors
~ Blue, yellow and some green

Aroma
~ Ylang-Ylang

Communication Bowl
~ Wooden or clay bowl or dish

Evoking Your Desire
~ On an un-lined piece of paper write a word or phrase that evokes your desire and put it into your communication bowl.

Devotional Blissiplines
~ Sacred Dance Meditation (*More bliss in chapter 6*)
~ On small pieces of paper, write down the things you love or admire about each other. Add them to your communication bowl throughout the week. At the end of the week, share and start again.

Placement Of Objects
~ Intention Symbol in the center of altar and your Communication Bowl in front of it. Candle and statue on the left side, flowers on the right.

Additional Items
~ Games, scavenger hunt, movie night

Health & Well-Being

Life can be challenging enough when everything is going great, but when you are not healthy, your perspective can shift into a dark place.

Making decisions to eat better, exercise and set goals for yourself, to live a more vibrant life are imperative decisions, but they can seem overwhelming.

An altar dedicated to your health can be a gentle way to take the first step.

98

HEALTH & WELL-BEING ALTAR EXAMPLE

Intention Symbol ~ Use a picture, make a collage or use words that inspire feelings of health and wellness.

Air ~ Standing wind chime, fan, feather

Earth ~ Statue of Quan Yin, or an aloe plant

Fire ~ Light blue or white candle in gold or glass holder

Water ~ Marigold plant or a fern in water

Fabric Colors ~ White, gold, green, and some pink

Aroma ~ Lavender

Communication Bowl ~ Gemstone or small glass bowl

Evoking Your Desires ~ Write a word or phrase that evokes the feelings you would like to experience and put it into your communication bowl.

Devotional Blissiplines ~ Body Awareness / Five Pointed Star Meditation (*More bliss in chapter 6*)
~ Do something for yourself everyday, do something compassionate and kind, spiritually or physically nurturing. (*Meditation, hot bath, massage, gentle walk, listen to up-lifting music*).
~ Use your Altars Of Intentions Cards.

Placement Of Objects ~ Intention Symbol in the center of altar and your Communication Bowl in front of it. Candle and statue on the left side, flowers and other objects on the right.

Additional Items ~ Turquoise Stone, medicine cards, prayer beads

Knowledge Or Creativity

Unlimited creativity and unbounded wisdom is available through the practice of opening up to higher consciousness with regular practices.

Learning not to get caught up in self- doubt will free up your energy, so you can create and gain more knowledge with confidence.

KNOWLEDGE OR CREATIVITY ALTAR EXAMPLE

Intention Symbol   ~ Make a Collage or use a book or picture

Air   ~ Standing wind chime, or fan

Earth   ~ Statue of Saraswati or Ganesh

Fire   ~ Yellow, or blue candle

Water   ~ Iris flowers or orange roses in a clear vase

Fabric Colors   ~ Blue, yellow, and some orange

Aroma   ~ Eucalyptus

Communication Bowl   ~ Small dish or silver tray

Evoking your Desires   ~ Write a word or phrase that evokes the feelings for the goal you wish to experience and put it into your communication bowl.

Devotional Blissiplines   ~ Acceptance Meditation (*More bliss in chapter 6*)
~ Delve deep into pondering, and then make a list of what it is that you really want to do, or know more about. Start with the one goal that has the most "pull" for you right now. Keep your list on your Altar.
~ Use your Altars Of Intentions Cards.

Placement Of Objects   ~ Intention Symbol in the center of altar and your Communication Bowl in front of it. Flowers and candle on the left side, statue or chimes on the right.

Additional Items   ~ Symbolic representations such as tarot cards, goddess cards or books. Amethyst Stone

Life Changes

In times of situations or experiences that appear beyond your control, remaining in balance and centered when you feel hurt, confused or burdened may seem out of reach. Using your altar as a solace and refuge can give you the comfort and the support that you deeply yearn for.

LIFE CHANGES ALTAR EXAMPLE

Intention Symbol ~ Use a Beautiful framed picture of Ganesh or make a collage or find a picture that inspire feelings of support and ease.

Air ~ Standing wind chimes, incense or feather

Earth ~ Conch shell, or statue of Tara

Fire ~ Red candle in a brass or gold container

Water ~ Red roses or orange roses

Fabric Colors ~ Silver, red and orange

Aroma ~ Fir

Communication Bowl ~ Brass dish or gem stone bowl

Evoking Your Desires ~ Write on a small unlined piece of paper a phrase or word that evokes the experience, solace or support you wish to receive, and put it into your communication bowl.

Devotional Blissiplines ~ Ground Yourself Meditation (*More bliss in chapter 6*)
~ Choose a card from your Altars Of Intentions deck. Use another deck that you may have and then do the sacred practice that the card suggests.

Placement Of Objects ~ Intention Symbol in the center of altar and your Communication Bowl in front. Candle and chimes on the left side, flowers and statue on the right.

Additional Items ~ Kali Statue, Citrine or Bloodstone

Relationship Or Marriage

What does love mean to you? Whatever the form of giving your heart to another takes, it is the willingness to gratefully receive from your existing relationships that will most quickly lead to understanding and fulfillment of your heart's desires.

RELATIONSHIP (or MARRIAGE) ALTAR EXAMPLE

Intention Symbol ~ Use a beautiful framed picture or collage that inspires a happy relationship that you desire.

Air ~ Standing wind chimes, incense, feathers

Earth ~ Two Rose Quartz crystals or a statue of Krishna

Fire ~ Two red floating candles in a crystal bowl, or two red candles in a glass votive, or two red candle holders.

Water ~ Clear crystal vase with fresh red roses or a small bowl with rose buds or petals floating in it.

Fabric Colors ~ Red, blue

Aroma ~ Ylang-Ylang

Communication Bowl ~ Clear glass or gemstone bowl

Evoking your Desires ~ Write on an unlined small piece of paper a word or phrase for the outcome that you desire and put it into your communication bowl.

Devotional Blissiplines ~ Sacred Dance Meditation (*More bliss in chapter 6*)
~ Write on small pieces of unlined paper, simple 15-30 minutes mini dates that can be done together for deeper connection. Take turns picking one daily to do.
~ Use your Altars Of Intentions Cards.

Placement Of Objects ~ Intention Symbol in the center of altar and your Communication Bowl in front. Statue and candle on the left side, flowers and other items on the right.

Additional Items ~ Moonstone Crystal, a book you are reading together.

Spirituality

Daily practices for your body, mind and spirit increases the harmony in your life. When you replenish your connection with the Divine, this spiritual nourishment calms the mind and brings peace.

SPIRITUALITY ALTAR EXAMPLE

Intention Symbol ~ Use a picture or statue of Buddha or make a collage that inspires your spiritual growth.

Air ~ Standing wind chime or a decorative fan

Earth ~ Potted sunflower, tulips or orchids

Fire ~ White candles, tea lights in clear votive

Water ~ Small table fountain, or floating flower petals

Fabric Colors ~ Gold, purple, and white

Aroma ~ Sandalwood

Communication Bowl ~ Small simple dish or brass tray

Evoking Your Desires ~ Write a phrase or word on a small unlined piece of paper that evokes the feelings you want to experience with the Divine. Put it into your communication bowl.

Devotional Blissiplines ~ Opening Your Heart (*More bliss in chapter 6*)
~ Use a guided meditation such as a chakra clearing, breath exercise or chanting daily.
~ Use your Altars Of Intentions Cards.

Placement Of Objects ~ Intention Symbol in the center of altar and your Communication Bowl in front. Flowers, crystals and statues on the left side, candles on the right.

Additional Items ~ Amethyst, religious symbols, book, smudge bowl

Travel Altar

When you are away from home, your intention and focus must remain strong.
Bring your altar with you if you plan to be gone for more than two days, so
that you can keep your Intentions and Blissiplines on track.
Create a sacred space anywhere you travel, by using the nightstand, coffee
table, or dresser to create your altar on.
Tip: Use small bags for your tea lights, smudge stick or bowl, and Intention Cards.

TRAVEL ALTAR EXAMPLE

Intention Symbol   ~ Use the Intention Symbol from your existing altar. If it is too big or heavy to pack, make a travel Intention Symbol. Using unlined paper cut out a heart shape. Write your desired outcome.

Air   ~ Small decorative fan, small bell or feather

Earth   ~ Semi-precious stones or a small statue

Fire   ~ Travel candles in a small tins with lids or a candle container and tea lights that are unbreakable.

Water   ~ Small unbreakable vase, or use a small plastic container/cup.

Fabric   ~ Silk scarf or a small piece of fabric

Communication Bowl   ~ Use the one from your home altar or bring an unbreakable small bowl/shell.

Evoking Your Desires   ~ Use the one from your existing altar

Devotional Blissiplines   ~ Bring your journal, spend time in nature, meditate, sacred dance, light your candles, use your Altars Of Intentions Cards or goddess cards.

Placement Of Objects   ~ Intention Symbol in the center of altar and your Communication Bowl in front of it. Candles on the left side, flowers and other items on your right.

Additional Items   ~ If you find something while traveling that adds to your intention and focus, you can rest it upon your altar. Maybe a special rock or a flower that you pick.

~ Resurrection ~

~ Transition ~

~ Growth ~

~ Healing ~

~ Grace ~

~ Soul ~

CHAPTER TWELVE
Igniting Your Altar

Step 10 ~ Ignite Your Altar

The altar igniting ceremony will help you to infuse positive energy and grace into what you are creating.

The ceremony begins with the most important law of manifestation: gratitude. Being grateful for what you have is essential for the success of your altar and the fulfillment of your dreams.

Another important key to the success of your sacred altar, and a part of the ceremony is, *openness*. Patient *openness* will act as the magnet that will manifest your intentions from your spirit and into reality.

It is best to be simple and clear in your requests to the Divine. Try not to limit yourself. If you don't ask, the answer is 'no.'
Your willingness to let go of all of your agendas, unbelievable expectations and outcomes, will lead to the fulfillment of your desires in surprising ways!

Remain humble, trusting and patient. Open your heart. Breathe.

True power and grace manifest through Infinite Consciousness. Using your altar and sacred ceremonies will magnetize transformation to happen.

Surrender to the Divine. Ask for joy, grace and ease.

A simple genuine prayer to the Divine is all that you need.
This empowering ceremony is for activating any sacred altar.

Before you begin, put on some beautiful music, light your candles, burn your incense, chime your bells, and prepare your heart.

Ceremony For Igniting Your Altar

~ Stand, kneel or sit in front of your sacred altar.

~ Hold an object, such as your *intention symbol*, which has importance to you.

~ Take a deep breath in, hold it and release, gently close your eyes.

~ Center yourself by opening your heart. You open your heart by simply intending to do so.

~ Imagine you are transferring your feelings, hopes, dreams, wishes and desires into the object you are holding. Imagine that you are infusing and igniting the object with your heart felt feelings.

~ Inhale a deep breath and imagine that you are breathing in *rose-colored contentment.* As you exhale, allow the *contentment* to flow throughout your body.

~ With the next inhale through your nose imagine that you are breathing in *rose-colored peace.* As you exhale, allow the *peace* to flow throughout your body.

~ Get a sense of how powerful and magical your altar will be for you. Hold this feeling, as you begin to recall the reasons you had for creating your sacred altar.

~ Now, imagine your desires and dreams forming a brilliant beam of intentions. See this beam leaving your heart and infusing everything on your altar with their meaning and feeling. Imagine with as much detail as possible, the successful fruition for all of your intentions for your sacred altar.

~ Envision your intention coming true. Merge with it. Become one with it. Build those feelings within your heart. Then, imagine that you are transferring the fullness of these feelings to your sacred altar.

~ Stay in this vision for a few minutes and *really feel it.* When you have completed the transmissions, place your right hand on your heart, then your left hand on top of it.

~ Take a few more breaths in, hold and release. With your last exhale release all the air with a sound. Be open to whatever sound naturally comes up and allow it to come out.

~ Now place your hands together in prayer position. Take one more deep breath in and release. When you are ready, open your eyes.

~ If you feel moved to do any sacred dance, movement or motion in front of your altar, do so. Meditate, pray or do whatever inspires you.

~ You may have another practice that has meaning for you, do it now, as this would further infuse your altar with more of you and your pure presence of light.

~ To end the ceremony, sit quietly in front of your sacred altar. Say to yourself, "it is done," and know that it is so.

~ Enjoy your altar and watch your desires come true.

Appreciation ~ Support ~ Time ~ Positive ~ Success

Appreciating Your Altar

Once your altar has been set up and ignited it begins to transmit the frequency of your desires. Everything you have created up to this point, from gathering all of your items, cleaning your space, and setting your intentions is now brought into a three-dimensional form.

Your attention, Blissiplines, appreciation and tending to your altar will help keep your dreams in harmony. Tend to your altar often by keeping it free from dirt and dust. Replace flowers and plants that are dying. Use smudge for clearing your altar, space and yourself.

After a few months, you may need to replace objects that no longer seem to be in alignment with your intended results. If you feel your altar is not producing the outcome that you are hoping for, take everything off and start the process over again. This time using some of the same items as you did before, touch everything with *love and appreciation.* As you gently handle your sacred objects, dusting each one, then replacing them upon your altar, deeply admire and transfer your sincere *heart felt* feelings. Do another ceremony for igniting your altar and be *open* to the materialized potential that this new sacred altar can gift. Be patient and trust that your connection with the Divine is potent and real.

Expression ~ Conscious ~ Intention ~ Connect ~ Divine

CHAPTER THIRTEEN
Sacred Dance

Sacred dance is as old as time. Sacred dance is natural spontaneous movement; it is a pure and instinctive devotion to the Divine. Dance awakens you to your beginnings, and to your real and true self. It is an expression of devotion. It is a way to return to your purpose and to awaken through movement.

Dance is a very natural part of life. Children dance easily. They are compelled to move spontaneously with or with out music. Teenagers dance to feel alive.

When you allow yourself to be relaxed, you can move more easily. Notice that your body is like a flowing wave, always in motion, moving with the energy around you. When you add music to the moment, it helps create rhythms, which can further encourage you out of your shell to express yourself. With practice, you learn, once again, to let go. When you let go and dance free, you are able to express your connection with the Divine.

You may need to playfully practice dancing to reach the point where you are in spontaneous free union with the Divine. But don't worry, the whole process of dance is sacred. Your efforts are sacred. Your inhibitions are sacred. Your shy and awkward feelings are sacred. Your triumphs are sacred.

So practice and play with your dancing. Allow the music to carry you away. Listen to the sounds and feel the instruments resonate in your body. You may feel the drums in your hips, the guitar in your spine. Begin with little movements until you feel relaxed enough to add more. Let the music and your feelings move you. Let go. Put it all together, and you will be move like the waves in the ocean – you will move without holding back.

When you experience freedom to flow with movement in your life, you will notice many precious insights. You will notice that grace and ease are natural. You will experience tremendous release and connectedness to self and others.

Sacred dance not only works on a physical level but it impacts you energetically and spiritually as well.

Through intentionally connecting to your body, you experience pleasure and joy as you express your true nature. You allow your divine light to shine.

If this movement feels weird, uncomfortable or useless, don't give up! Try something new. Embrace the experience as best you can. Don't judge yourself or the occurrence. Relax and be with it.

Be willing to be humble. View your private sacred dance as a precious opportunity to be free and to be with the Divine. Once you have finished, give yourself praise. Yes, praise! The feminine in you grows through praise – even if it comes from yourself.

You deserve praise, and you need to honor yourself with it. Sacred dance is your divine opportunity to give yourself some loving praise. Just let go and dance your way past old barriers that no longer serve you.

Here is a truthful secret: Within you there is a divine goddess, and that part of you yearns for soulful movement. Once you try it you will feel your heart begin to bloom open.

Can you hear it? Can you hear the gentle quiet voice within, coaxing you to *move*? You may be surprised to discover that it will not only fulfill your life, but the magical results of your sacred dancing will somehow reach beyond you, to touch the lives of others too! You won't be able to prove it wrong. Sacred dance changes everything – for the better!

So, dance! Move for *your* sake and for the sake of others.
The practice of devotional dance will become one of your Spiritual practices (A Devotional Blissipline). The sacred-ness of your dance will bring you the connection with the universal dancer that you have always craved.

Sacred ~ Dancing ~ Movement ~ Connect ~ Intentions

Sacred Dance is a way of radiating love through movement. When choosing your music, mix it up. Learn to dance and move to almost anything.

It is good to have music that moves you in such a way that whatever comes through your dance is just what your body needed to release. Once you take on this practice, you will find that you will be able to dance and to 'be' with anything.

SACRED MUSIC MENU

Aurambolia
Dreamland (Live in the Jungle)

Barglee Thomas
Culpa

Donna De Lory
Bathe In These Waters

Drum Sex
Dinner At The Sugarbush

Eric Bibb
Spirit I Am

Etta James
At Last

India Arie
Break the Shell, Soulbird Rise

Jaya Lasshmi
Jewel Of Hari

Karunesh
Joy Of Life-Return Of The Rains

Kaya Project
So It Goes, Dark Road

Mercan Dede
Senaname On Seychatname

Michael Franti
Yes I will

Miten with Deva Palma
So Much Magnificence

Putunago Asia
Dreams of Happiness

RanachandraRadhaPranam
By Your Grace

Sade
By Your Side

Shamans Dream World Groove Ensemble
Lalla's Ecstacy on Tribo Musica

Snatam Kaur
By Thy Grace

Snatam Kaur
Mul Mantra

Steven Halpern
Chakra Suite

Stevie Winwood
Higher Love

Wayne Dyer And James Tyman
Moses Code Meditation

Whitney Houston
The Greatest Love of All

Cleanse ~ Protect ~ Banish ~ Release ~ Bless ~

Cleanse your altars often with a quick smudge and a blessing for what is going on in your life at the time. As you work with your altar, you will intuitively grow to know how often you need to cleanse. You may want to specifically create your own personal energy balancing and clearing ceremonies by using a positive affirmation or a mental image of a safe and nurturing environment.

Avoid over doing it with the smoke – a little goes a long way. Your intentions are the most important component of this spiritual ceremony.

CHAPTER FOURTEEN
Smudging With Cedar And Sage

The effects of smudging can happen surprisingly swiftly and can be wonderfully dramatic. Smudging can quickly turn any space into an unassuming and soothing sanctuary.

There are many ways to use sacred smudge sticks and smudge bowls. The uses may include: cleansing, blessing, protecting, banishing, releasing, supporting and more.

The three blessings described in this chapter are for 1) Cleansing yourself, 2) Cleansing another person, and 3) Cleansing space, such as a room, home or sacred altar.

Cleansing through smudging drives away negativity and puts you and your space into a state of balance.

You will need a smudge stick, a bowl or seashell and a large feather. If you do not have a feather, you may use your hand to waft the smoke in the beginning.

Eventually, you will want to purchase – or better yet to find – a feather to cleanse your space and altar. The feather represents maintaining your balance no matter how the winds of life may blow.

You may buy a smudge stick from a store or make your own. Making your own smudge stick will require more effort in collecting the fresh herbs, but it allows you a deeper connection with the spirits of the sacred plants that are used in the smudge. There are eight steps in this book to make your own smudge stick.

If possible, collect your sage, cedar and herbs from the wild, when they are blooming. Always approach the plant with great respect. Perhaps ask the spirits of the plants for permission to use them for your healing smudge. Asking will better connect you to the Spirit that lives in all things. In turn, this will help your smudge to feel more meaningful, which will make it powerful for you.

SACRED HERBS

Cedar
Clears Negative Emotions
Offers Healing

Dried Red Roses
Love
Desire

Dried White Roses
Purify
Unconditional Love

Dried Yellow Roses
Friendship
Joy

Garlic
Protection
Immunity

Ginger
Strength
Potent Vitality

Juniper
Purification
Safety & Sacredness – Especially for Space

Lavender
Restores Balance
Loving Energy

Mug Wort
Banishes Evil Spirits
Restores Balance

Rosemary
Brings Clarity
Rejuvenates

Sage
Wisdom
Healing

Sagebrush
Aides Change
Transforms Energy

Sweet Grass
Attracts Positive Energy
Clears Negativity

Yerba Santa
Protects Boundaries
Purification

Items Needed To Create A Smudge Stick

* Cedar and Sage ~ 3 - 4 sprigs each, 6 inches short stick. 12 inches long stick
* Lavender Stalks with Buds ~ 8 - 10 pieces each, 6-8 inches long tied together
* Small Dried Herbs ~ 1 teaspoon each
* Dried Rose Petals ~ 8-10
* Colored Embroidery Thread ~ 12 ft. long and double it - total of 6 ft. per stick
* Sharp Scissors & Small Trimming Scissors
* Small Shell/Symbol ~ With a 'hole' in it to string thread through it. (*Optional*)
* Candles
* Lighter
* Sacred Music

Smudge Stick Making Ceremony

You may want some music that will enhance your experience. Once all of your materials are gathered, light your candles and begin.

~ With your intention, call in the Spirits to cleanse and protect.

~ Bring a piece of your sage and/or cedar up to your nose to smell, as you close your eyes, take a deep inhale in, and slowly release it.

~ Holding your sage/cedar piece in your hands, as if your hands are a sacred bowl. With your next inhale, intend for your spirit to connect with this sacred plant.

~ As you exhale say, "I am connecting with this sacred plant."

~ Take another breath in, and as you exhale, release any negative emotions you may have.

~ Relax as you breathe. Just be in this moment.

~ On your final inhale, imagine breathing in all of the wisdom this sacred plant has to gift you. As you exhale, allow yourself to feel the new awareness you received from this Sacred Smudge making ceremony.

~ Bring your hands to your heart. First, place your right hand on your heart. Next, place your left hand on top of your right hand. To complete, say, "Thank you," aloud when you are ready. You are done. Your sage and cedar is ready for binding.

HOW TO MAKE A SMUDGE STICK

Step 1:
Gather all of your items, measure, cut and arrange everything, so it is ready to go. On your table lay down a piece of cedar or sage branch. Take your lavender stick, sage and place them together in the center of the cedar/sage branch. If you want to add dried herbs, sprinkle them in at this point. Cover the whole thing with another sprig or two of cedar or sage. As you arrange all of the branches, sprigs and grasses, make sure that the stems all line up at the bottom.

Step 2:
Before you pick up your bundle, wrap the thread you have prepared about one inch from the bottom and tie a knot to hold your bundle together.

Step 3:
Using your non - dominant hand, hold the bundle, as if you were holding a bouquet, and with your other hand wrap the thread *firmly* around the base 4-6 times to hold the ends together. When you begin wrapping your bundle, do so at a slight slant, holding it firmly as you work your way up the bundle.

Step 4:
As you wrap the thread around your bundle, allow one inch between each wrap. Wind the thread up the stick eight to nine times until you arrive about 3 inches from the top. Place *rose petals* on your stick anywhere you want them as you wind your thread up and down the bundle. The thread will hold the petals in place.

Step 5:

Be sure to hold the thread *firmly*, as you crisscross your way back down. The thread will be forming an **X** design as you wrap it eight to nine more times. Anchor some more of the *rose petals* as you wind your way down your stick.

Step 6:

Wrap any left over thread around the bottom of your newly formed smudge stick 4-5 times and tie it off with a few knots. Shape the top of your smudge stick leaving a few sprigs of lavender sticking out. Trim the entire stick, being careful not to cut your thread.

Step 7:
Use a pair of sharp scissors to cut off the end of your smudge stick to give it a clean finished look. You may use your left over cedar/sage and lavender sprigs for a smudging shell/bowl.

Step 8:
If you would like to add a small shell or any other symbol, you can tie it on with your leftover thread. Hang your smudge stick upside down to dry in a warm/dry place for 5-6 days. Once it is dry you may smudge your altar, yourself, another person and your sacred space.

Tips:

    ~ This can be a messy project so choose a work area that is easy to clean.

    ~ It is best to use fresh cedar and sage so when binding, it is easier to manage and less likely to break apart.

    ~ If you don't have enough thread at the end to tie on a small shell, simply wrap around another 4-5 inches of new thread onto the bottom of the smudge stick, and tie it off with a knot. Then you can add your chosen shell or token symbol.

    ~ Be patient and take your time, it will always be just right.

Positive ~ Energy ~ Purify ~ Clarity ~ Healing ~ Wisdom

Smudging Ceremony

~ Light the candles on your altar.

~ Light the end of your smudge stick, and let it burn until the tips begin to smolder. Use your feather or hand to further ignite the smudge stick and to keep it burning.

~ With your intention, call in Divine Spirit to cleanse and to protect.

~ Say, "I use this Sacred Divine Sage to clear away all negativity from my heart and anything else unworthy and impure."

~ You may say this either quietly to yourself or out loud. Say it with heart so the universe can receive your wish.

~ See and believe that all negative thoughts, emotions and energies are lifting away.

~ Holding the smudge stick in front of you, use the feather or you other hand to waft the smoke towards your heart.

~ Take the smudge stick over your head, then down both of your arms, and down the front of your body.

~ Next, guide the smoke down the back of your body towards the ground.

~ Say to yourself the following intention: "All negativity is being taken into the Earth."

~ As you smudge, imagine yourself surrounded by *loving energy*. Feel your emotions. Breathe in love.

Always smudge yourself before clearing others. When you smudge someone else have them sit or stand. Use the same procedure on them that you used on yourself. Have the person repeat all of words and intentions. When you are done, thank them for the honor.

Four Directions Ceremony

Sacred smudge clearing is a great way to move stagnant energy from any room in your home or an area that needs cleansing. If your life feels stuck or things aren't going in the right direction, a simple space clearing will do the trick.

~ Light your smudge stick and have your shell/bowl with you. Stand in the center of your space, and with each direction fan the smudge four times as you call in the Great Spirit.

~ Turn to the East in the room, and fan smudge out into that direction four times, saying: "Great Spirit of Air, cleanse and inspire this space. Thank you."

~ Turn to the South. Say: "Great Spirit of Water, strengthen and bring peace to this space. Thank you."

~ Turn to the West. Say: "Great Spirit of Fire, protect and energize this space. Thank you."

~ Turn to the North. Say: "Great Spirit of Earth, cleanse and ground this space. Thank You."

~ Look up to the Heavens, sending smudge up towards that direction. Say: "Great Father Sky, guard this space from above. Thank you."

~ Kneel towards the ground and fan smudge down into the Earth. Say: "Great Mother Earth, nurture this space with Divine Love. Thank you."

~ Take your burning smudge stick, and put it out in your smudge shell. Be sure the fire is out. Place the smudge stick on your altar. Close your eyes. Say: "Thank you Divine Directions (and add a final blessing in your own words – whatever you feel moved to say)."

~ When you are ready, open your eyes and feel the Divine gift you are and will always be. You are strong. You are full of energy and inspiration.

Sacred Smudge Bowl or Shell

Smudge bowls are just as common as smudge sticks. If you prefer or if you are unable to get fresh herbs, you may want to use a smudge bowl instead of a smudge stick.

Both tools are equally powerful. They are both easy to use, store and make. It is up to you, which smudge tool to utilize.

You may use your smudge bowl for the same purposes as you would use a smudge stick. To use a smudge bowl, light the dried herbs and grasses in the bowl. Holding the bowl in one hand, use your other hand to hold your feather. Move your feather to direct the smoke towards you, someone else or wherever you intend the smoke to travel. Trust your intuition how much you need to use for each smudging ceremony.

Items Needed to Make Your Smudge Bowl

* Dried Herbs/Sage/Cedar/Rose Petals ~ 2 - 3 Tablespoons Each
* Seashell ~ 1 Large Clam, Abalone or Oyster Shell
* Bowl, if not using a shell ~ One that can withstand heat
* Self-Igniting Charcoal Blocks ~ Several – (*Optional*)
* Measuring Spoon ~ 1 Tablespoon
* Feather ~ 1 Large
* Matches or Lighter ~ 1 of your choice
* Sacred Music ~ Your Choice

~ Heart ~

~ Cleanse ~

~ Protect ~

~ Remove ~

~ Harmony ~

~ Balance ~

Smudge Bowl Making Ceremony

~ Gather all of your materials to make your smudge bowl.

~ Light your candle and center yourself. Take a few slow deep breaths to bring yourself to this 'here and now' moment.

~ Using a Tablespoon, scoop each of your chosen herbs/grasses and mix them together in your bowl/shell.

~ With your intention, call in the Spirits to cleanse and protect.

~ Hold your shell/bowl with both of your hands. Close your eyes. Take a deep cleansing breath in, hold it, and release.

~ With your next inhale, hold your shell up in the air towards the sky and say: "Sacred Divine, use this sage to clear away all negativity from my heart and anything else that is unworthy or impure."

~ Take a few more cleansing breaths and say: "Thank You Sacred Spirit."

~ Inhale one more deep cleansing breath and as you exhale, let the vibration of your voice flow out with sound.

~ When you are ready, open your eyes.

Room Smudging Ceremony

~ Light your candle and center yourself. Take a deep breath in and exhale.

~ Feel your heart and say your intention: "I ask for harmony and balance to be restored to this room and to my altar."

~ Begin to walk around the room wafting smoke from your lit smudge stick or bowl with a feather into each corner of the room and then over your altar.

~ Say these words: "Great Spirits, cleanse, protect and remove negative energies from this space."

~ Repeat this process until you feel that the room is clear.

Beauty And Your Senses

Essential oils and incense can be used for much more than a mood enhancer. There are hundreds of healing purposes and ways to use them. For the purpose of your sacred altar, create your own blends to add the healing qualities that can help support and manifest your desires.

You may also add oils to a spray mister for spraying your space, your bed sheets, your pillows or anything you like.

When you need a 'pick-me-up' while you are away from home, add 1-3 drops of your chosen oil to a tissue or handkerchief so you can sniff as needed. Note: To avoid damage, do not spray any wood in your home.

CHAPTER FIFTEEN
Essential Oils And Incense

Aromatherapy can bring support, balance and harmony to your body and to your emotions. Healing essential oils are most commonly extracted from varieties of trees, shrubs, herbs, grasses and flowers via a process called steam distillation.

The steam from the process contains the essential essences. When it cools, the oil is separated from the water and filtered to become essential oils.

There are a large variety of essential oils, which you can incorporate into your rituals and into your daily life. There are many practical guidebooks, which can help you align your personal needs with the essences available. Beyond that, your intuition will serve you well. You will be drawn to use the essences you need for healing or clearing your space.

Once you have chosen the oil or a blend of oils, you may use an aromatherapy burner to fill the room with your choice. Ceramic or soapstone diffusers are the most popular.

Note: Essential oils are potent medicine and should not be used directly on your skin, unless diluted first.

HEALING OILS

Bay
Brings Wisdom
Peace, Protection

Cardamom
Helps with Impotence
Raises Low Sexual Response

Cedar
Stimulates the Pineal Gland
Calming, Purifying

Chamomile
Helps with Impatience or Feeling Disagreeable
PMS

Cinnamon
Boosts Brain, Ease Nervous Tension, Increases Memory
Helps with Pain

Clove
Provides Physical and Emotional Insight
Improves Memory

Eucalyptus
Inhalants and Vapor Rubs
Soothes Nausea

Fir
Helps with Fatigue
Soothes Muscular Aches and Pains

Frankincense
Symbolizes Divinity, Promotes Balance
Offers Protection, Fortitude, Courage, Resolution, Spiritual Awareness, Inspiration

Geranium
Balances Emotions, Lifts Depression
Keeps away Negative Energies

Ginger
Supports the Digestive System
An Aphrodisiac

Jasmine
Helps Boost Confidence, Reduces Fear and Anxiety
Brings out Feelings of Love

Juniper
Protection, Supports in Difficult Times, Stimulates the Mind
Raises Self-Esteem

Lavender
Heals, Purifies, Balances, Soothes
Peaceful Sleep, Eases Stress, Aids Resolution in Difficult Times

Lemon
Lifts Spirits
Helps with Acceptance, Release and Letting Go

Lime
Cleanses the Aura
Renews the Spirit

Myrrh
Spiritually Purifying and Restorative
Aids Meditation

Myrtle
Emblem of Love, Uplifting and Euphoric
Balances Male and Female Energies of the Body

Nutmeg
Supports the Nervous and Endocrine Systems
Boosts Energy

Patchouli
Erotic Aroma
Cleansing and Reviving

Peppermint
Memory, Emotions
Circulation, Awareness

Pine
Helps the Mind – Mental Clarity
Concentration and Memory Loss

Rosemary
Remedy for Depression, Mental Fatigue, Memory
Helps to Refresh Energy

Sage
Balances Hormones in Men and Women
Enhances Spiritual Awareness

Sandalwood
Meditation, Insomnia, Anxiety
Release the Past, Ease Transition

Sweet Almond
Direct Therapeutic Effect, Aids Lungs, Decongestant

Sweet Orange
Cheers the Heart, Brightens the Mood
Positive Energy to the Atmosphere

Tea Tree
Helps with Infection
Anti-fungal, Anti-viral, Anti-bacterial

Ylang-Ylang
Enhancement for Love and Sex
Promotes Confidence

CREATING MAGIC OILS

Bath
3 Tbsp. Sweet Almond or Avocado Oil + 20 drops Lavender Oil
Mix
Use one tsp. per bath

Death
2 drops each Sandalwood Oil + 2 drops Juniper Oil
Mix
Burn in your oil burner

Igniting Your Altar
3 drops Juniper Oil + 3 drops Lavender Oil
Mix
Burn in your oil burner

Love
2 drops Ylang-Ylang Oil
Mix
Burn in your oil burner

Massage
6 drops of your chosen Oil(s) + 4 tsp. of Sweet Almond or Apricot Kernel Oil
Mix
Use liberally for massage

Party Mood Enhancer
3 drops Lemon Oil + 3 drops Orange Oil
Mix
Burn in your oil burner

Senses – Stimulating
5 oz. distilled water + 1 tsp. Olive Oil + 6 drops Rosemary Oil
1 sprig Fresh Rosemary
Add to spray bottle
Shake well to mix
Spritz on damp clean skin

Separation or Divorce
3 drops Lemon Oil + 3 drops Lavender Oil
Mix
Burn in your oil burner

Smudge Sticks
Dab your smudge stick *very lightly* (Using a tissue)
Use any oil that has the affect you intend

Water Bowl
5-9 drops each of a mix of Oils
Bring kettle water to a boil
Fill small bowl with hot water and add drops of your favorite Oil(s)

BASIC OIL BLENDING

Citrus
Orange + Lemon + Lime

Earthy
Patchouli + Sage

Eastern
Ginger + Patchouli

Floral
Lavender + Jasmine

Medicinal
Eucalyptus + Tea Tree

Minty
Peppermint + Spearmint

Spicy
Nutmeg + Clove + Cinnamon

Woodsy
Pine + Cedar + Sage

Stimulates ~ Balances ~ Soothes ~ Cleanses ~ Restores

A great way for dispersing your healing essences is to fill a small bowl with hot kettle water. Add 5-9 drops of oil(s) to the water, and it will fill your room with magic. Perhaps add oil into your bath for a relaxed mood or add some essence to your massage oil for a wonderful way to end a stressful day.

Pleasure ~ Ritual ~ Healing ~ Meditation

There are many benefits in using incense. Incense is known to reduce
depression, anxiety, dissipate negative energy and purify the air.
Incense can soothe the mind, kill bacteria and create a positive atmosphere.

Incense

Incense is an aromatic material, which releases fragrant smoke when burned. It is used for a variety of purposes including religions, spirituality, aromatherapy, meditation, repel insects and for simple pleasure.

Using incense as part of your altar Devotional Blissiplines adds the *fire element* and can also benefit your space by the healing properties associated with it.

The "Incense Effects Chart" will give you suggestions for the aroma that can support your desired intentions.

There are four basic forms of incense: stick, cone, loose and cylinder. The unique aroma of any incense comes from the various woods and resins used to give the incense its scent and properties.

To find out the best fragrance for you, it is fun to try an incense sample kit. Watch for your emotional responses, while the incense burns.

Be aware not to buy the cheapest incense available, as these products often contain unhealthy chemicals.

For the most part, incense is pure and natural.

INCENSE EFFECTS

Cleansing
Cedar, Clove, Gold Copal, Juniper, Pine, Rosemary, Sage, Sweet Grass

Courage, Strength, Confidence
Rose, Peppermint, Musk, Gardenia, Frankincense

Creativity
Clove, Dream Herb, Star Anise, Frankincense

Hormones
Geranium, Jasmine

Meditation And Prayer
Aloe, Benzoin, Black Copal, Cedar, Dammar

Mood Swings
Geranium, Lemon, Mandarin Orange, Tuberose

Prosperity And Wealth
Allspice, Aloe, Basil, Cedar, Sage, Poppy, Oak Moss, Nutmeg, Mint

Relaxation
Aloe, Amber, Anise, Cinnamon

Sacred Sanctuary Ambience
African Violet, Chamomile, Sandalwood

Sensuous
Ylang-Ylang, Patchouli, Rose, Lotus, Jasmine, Cardamom

Sleep
Amber, Cinnamon, Dream Herb

Spiritual Well-Being And Inner Peace
Lavender, Lemon, Lilac, Sandalwood, Pine

Ward Off Negative Forces
Bergamot, Carnation, Eucalyptus, Juniper, Frankincense, Ginseng

Yoga
Amber

The Glossary section is to help clarify some of the
meanings and terms used in this sacred altar book.

GLOSSARY

Air Element
Movement, change and attraction

Abalone Shell
May be used to hold smudge stick ashes or a loose mix of cedar and sage

Altar
An intentionally crafted structure or environment, where ceremonies and intentions take place

Anchor
A source of stability or security

Bells
A symbolically divine protective sound that carries you beyond your mind and reaches into your soul

Blissiplines
An intentional practice you choose to do, to reach closer to your goals and ideas

Collage
A work of art composed of photographs, magazine clippings, ribbons, yarn, fabric and objects attached to a background of some kind

Chimes
To call, welcome or clear the space

Communication Bowl
A bowl or container to place symbols or words for your intentions

Conch Shell
A shell used to represent the five elements: earth, water, fire, air and space

Deity
A God, Goddess or Divine Being

Devotional
The act of devoting or the state of being devoted

Divine
The underlying sustaining and creative force of the Universe

Drums
Can be used for sacred ceremony

Earth Element
Grounding influence; support and strength

Evoke
To call upon something, assistance, or higher power

Feather
Represents maintaining balance

Fire Element
Transformation, forward movement and change

Focus
Close or narrow attention; concentration

Gongs
Represents a powerful message from the subconscious

Incense
Used for purity and incorruptibility

Intentions
A course of acting, an objective/an aim, which guides action, intent, purpose to reach a goal

Manifest
Reveal, present or make apparent

Meditation
A practice of relaxation and of training the mind to induces a mode of consciousness

Rattles
Can be used for physical healing and to summon the spirits for the four directions

Ritual
A rite or ceremonial procedure

Sacred Dance
Encompasses all movement that expresses or enhances spiritual experiences

Singing Bowl
Made from brass, emits tones that set up a response, which create a balance between the right and left sides of the brain

Sea Salt
A natural purifier used to cleanse sacred crystals and stones

Shell
Used to hold cedar and sage for smudging
Feminine symbol for love, fertility, and source of life

Vision Board
A collage of images of things you want to experience in your life

Divine Thank You
Science of Being ~ 'Star Exercise'
Coffee and Clay ~ 'Finger Plates'
Harmony Integration ~ 'Breakthrough Journey'

For more information on the other healing modalities including the Breakthrough Journeys that Brenda has to offer, visit her web site at www.yourdivinepathway.com

Altars Of Intentions Cards, Meditation Eye Pillows, Cedar & Sage Sticks and Communication Bowls are also available.

Inspiration ~ Vitality ~ Flexibility ~ Gentleness ~ Heart

Message From Brenda

"As you become more clear who you really are, you'll be better able to decide what is best for you, the first time around. ~ Oprah Winfrey ~

This quote says it all to me. I have spent many years to begin to discover who I really am. The more I do discover my *True Self*, the more I want to help others to do the same.

My book, intention cards and my healing facilitation practice is the natural result of my own spiritual journey and my deep desire to see others' dreams come true. For the past decade, I have used Sacred Altars to *focus* my *intentions,* to bring about my goals and dreams. These precious and truly sacred spaces have given me the fortitude, courage, and clarity to follow through and fulfill my hearts desire.

My PHP (Pretty Hats Profile)

* Native Girl ~ Born and raised in the Pacific Northwest (Seattle)
* Devoted Wife ~ Married to Sean since 1989
* Proud Mom ~ Two amazing grown sons, Brett and Drew
* Loyal Friend ~ Active part in my community
* Dancer ~ Letting life dance me
* Sacred Space and Altar Designer ~ Gifts of creation, healing and manifestation
* Musician ~ Fourth generation Harpist
* Education Seeker ~ Attended and staffed many personal growth events
* Photographer ~ Amateur picture taker and professional beauty seeker
* Fisherwoman ~ Dedicated to family fun
* Gardener ~ Grower of vegetables, flowers and dreams
* Hiker ~ Avid fan of walking the earth
* Family Member ~ Always involved personally and professionally
* Business Women ~ Family Door Company Assistant
* Tide Flat Walker ~ Appreciating life in every breath
* Bird Lover ~ Mother to our bird, Merlin
* Friend of Bill W. ~ Since 1987
* Lavender and Sage Expert ~ Understanding properties of healing and clearing
* Arts and Crafts ~ Always creating and playing
* World Traveler ~ More traveling is on my 'bucket list'

Removes Obstacles ~ Offering Wisdom ~ Prosperity

Made in the USA
San Bernardino, CA
17 December 2014